MARRIAGE WAS MADE FOR MAN

MARRIAGE
WAS MADE FOR MAN

*A Study of the Problem of
Marriage and Divorce in relation to
the Church of England*

BY

A. P. SHEPHERD
D.D. *Canon of Worcester*

METHUEN & CO LTD
36 ESSEX STREET · LONDON WC2

First published 1958
© *A. P. Shepherd 1958*
Printed and bound in Great Britain
by The Camelot Press, Southampton
Catalogue No 6113/U

Contents

Foreword by the Bishop of Worcester

※

This is a controversial book. It is bound to be, because the subject is a controversial one—in fact, no marriage breaks up unless there has first been a controversy—but Dr Shepherd's real concern is not with principles as theories, but as they affect persons. He is a pastor of great experience and has, I know, helped many by his sympathetic understanding of their problems. His object in writing is to offer help where help is most badly needed, and I am grateful to him for asking me to write a brief introduction because I believe this is a book which needed to be written and should most certainly be read, for if Marriage was made for Man, all of us are either its product or its participants. And if Marriage was made for Man, by whom was it made? Our Lord's answer to this, as recorded in Mark's Gospel, is both clear and decisive. God created the sexes complementary to each other to be united in the marriage bond. Husband and wife become one flesh, and from an ideal point of view marriage is then indissoluble. But Christ seems to allow that divorce has to be recognized as an accommodation to a rude state of society—'Moses because of the hardness of your hearts suffered you to put away your wives; but from the beginning it was not so'—a state which certainly exists today. Eric Linklater writes of 'the great vulgar sin of these dishevelled times —hardness of heart'.

Marriage was Made for Man

Our concern then should be to uphold Christ's ideal of and for marriage, and at the same time to imitate His charity towards those who fail to do so; and it is unfortunate that when Christians consider the matter, they often seem more concerned to score debating points than to help those whose marriages have been broken. Liberals look upon rigorists with horror as those who submerge compassion and love under rules and regulations, while rigorists appear to regard any who do not share their attitude as either non-moral or at best sloppy sentimentalists. But no marriage is ever broken except after much suffering, and for those who have experienced the bitterness of disillusion and unfulfilled hopes, the Christian attitude should be one of sympathy, not censoriousness.

The value of Dr Shepherd's book is its positive approach to the problems of marriage. He states clearly his beliefs and the reasons for them, and then goes on to suggest ways in which those who desire to make a second marriage can do so within the fellowship of the Church and by the help of the means of grace. Here it is surely worth remembering that the sacraments were not ordained to be the private privilege of the perfect, but to help sinners to be better children of God, who is the loving Father of us all. Dr Shepherd, however, does not deal only with the question of divorce and remarriage; he is concerned with reforms both in the preparation for marriage and in the service itself, which would encourage a couple whose marriage seemed to be going astray to consult the Church first and only see the Divorce Court as a last desperate remedy.

But if the Church is to help people in this way, it will most certainly have to equip the clergy to do so. Pastoral counselling is an art in itself, and those who give it must be men who are themselves free from prejudice, integrated personalities, and who have knowledge both of Moral Theology and Psychology, for the true pastor must deal with every case on its merits. He must hold in balance both the justice and the love of God, and he must know just how much to be involved with, and how much to be detached from, those whom he is trying to help. I do not believe that every parish priest has these particular gifts, and if such a plan as Dr Shepherd envisages is to succeed, all cases will have to be referred to the Bishop and certain counsellors selected by him, and moreover there will have to be some agreed pattern, which every Diocese will accept.

Dr Shepherd takes very strong exception to the Regulations of Convocation on the question of the re-marriage in Church of the divorced, but I must confess myself that I have always found them both practical and wise. I speak from the experience of the last ten years, first as Vicar of a central London church where, alas, we were dealing with marriage problems daily, and secondly as a diocesan Bishop. When properly explained these regulations are not resented, but are usually appreciated as showing that the Church cares for the needs of particular cases and yet upholds the standards of her Master. But they must be explained *in love*, and whenever it is reasonably possible to admit anyone to the fellowship of the Church I would always do so. I believe in discipline, but it would appear from the gospel that discipline was designed for the selfish, the proud, the gossiper, and the jealous, and not merely for those who have broken their marriage vows. And here I must confess that I dislike the use of the term 'Innocent Party' in a discussion of this nature. I know what it means, but it is an unfortunate expression. In my experience the words 'innocent' and 'guilty', as used in the Divorce Court, are technical terms, and more often than not have little moral significance. We are none of us innocent; we are in fact a Communion of Sinners struggling to become a Communion of Saints. It is only when we can take our failures, whether in marriage or anything else, to the cross of Christ and seek there forgiveness that we can hope to find God's remedy for the hardness of our hearts.

I commend this book, because it will make us think, and the more we think, the better we can pray. And it is only rational thought and prayer that will remove the prejudices which surround these problems on every side, and lead us to find a solution which we can believe is in accordance with the mind of Him who made marriage for man.

MERVYN WORCESTER

Act of Convocation

CONVOCATION OF CANTERBURY
REGULATIONS CONCERNING MARRIAGE AND DIVORCE

passed in the Upper House on 16 May, 1956, and 23 May, 1957, and in the Lower House on 21, 22, and 23 May, 1957:

I 'That this House reaffirms the following four Resolutions of 1938, and in place of Resolution 5 then provisionally adopted by the Upper House substitutes Resolution 2(A) below, which restates the procedure generally followed since 1938.'

(1) 'That this House affirms that according to God's will, declared by Our Lord, marriage is in its true principle a personal union, for better or for worse, of one man with one woman, exclusive of all others on either side, and indissoluble save by death.'

(2) 'That this House also affirms as a consequence that re-marriage after divorce during the lifetime of a former partner always involves a departure from the true principle of marriage as declared by our Lord.'

(3) 'That in order to maintain the principle of lifelong obligation which is inherent in every legally contracted marriage and is expressed in the plainest terms in the Marriage Service the Church should not allow the use of that Service in the case of anyone who has a former partner still living.'

13

(4) 'That while affirming its adherence to our Lord's principle and standard of marriage as stated in the first and second of the above resolutions, this House recognizes that the actual discipline of particular Christian Communions in this matter has varied widely from time to time and place to place, and holds that the Church of England is competent to enact such a discipline of its own in regard to marriage as may from time to time appear most salutary and efficacious.'

2(A) 'Recognizing that the Church's pastoral care for all people includes those who during the lifetime of a former partner contract a second union, this House approves the following pastoral regulations as being the most salutary in present circumstances:

(a) When two persons have contracted a marriage in civil law during the lifetime of a former partner of either of them, and either or both desire to be baptized or confirmed or to partake of the Holy Communion, the incumbent or other priest having the cure of their souls shall refer the case to the Bishop of the diocese, with such information as he has and such recommendations as he may desire to make.

(b) The Bishop in considering the case shall give due weight to the preservation of the Church's witness to Our Lord's standard of marriage and to the pastoral care of those who have departed from it.

(c) If the Bishop is satisfied that the parties concerned are in good faith and that their receiving of the Sacraments would be for the good of their souls and ought not to be a cause of offence

14

to the Church, he shall signify his approval thereof both to the priest and to the party or parties concerned: this approval shall be given in writing and shall be accepted as authoritative both in the particular diocese and in all other dioceses of the province.'

2(B) 'No public Service shall be held for those who have contracted a civil marriage after divorce. It is not within the competence of the Convocations to lay down what private prayers the curate in the exercise of his pastoral Ministry may say with the persons concerned, or to issue regulations as to where or when these prayers shall be said.'

2(C) 'Recognizing that pastoral care may well avert the danger of divorce if it comes into play before legal proceedings have been started, this House urges all clergy in their preparation of couples for marriage to tell them, both for their own sakes and for that of their friends, that the good offices of the clergy are always available.'

In the Convocation of Canterbury meeting in Full Synod on 1 October, 1957, the President (the Archbishop of Canterbury) declared the above Resolutions to be an Act of Convocation.

I

Introduction

The relationship between man and woman is an issue of more universal interest than almost any other. This has always been so, but never so completely and consciously as it is today. In the popular press it is the most dominant news-item, while there is hardly a book, or play, or film in which it is not a major issue.

From the point of view of society and religion it presents itself in the question of marriage and divorce, and there we find one factor of the greatest interest, namely, the utter diversity of opinion on this question held by people of the highest moral integrity. This difference of opinion does not only exist between those who regard the matter as merely a social problem—albeit one of the highest importance and most far-reaching consequences —and those who see it as a religious and spiritual issue, governed by the mind and teaching of Jesus Christ. Even amongst the professed followers of Christ there is wide difference of opinion as to what that loyalty involves, and wide diversity of official practice between Christian Churches. The Eastern Orthodox Church allows divorce on certain grounds, and the remarriage, under conditions, of both parties. The Roman Church declares marriage to be indissoluble and prohibits divorce. Most of the Protestant Churches recognize divorce on certain grounds

16

embodied in State law and permit remarriage, and the Established Church of Scotland has followed that rule for 300 years. The Church of England, which for 100 years has rather indeterminately tolerated divorce and permitted the remarriage of those who are divorced, has now reverted to a more rigorous attitude and discipline.

This more rigorous approach by the Church of England has not only brought this issue prominently before the public, but it has also created a division of opinion in the minds of church people that will not easily be settled. Although Convocation has drawn up regulations and a form of discipline in regard to remarriage after divorce as an Act of Convocation, the fact remains that, in spite of this, there is a sense of uneasiness in many quarters in the Church. It is only in the Convocations that the matter has been fully discussed, and to some extent in the House of Laity of the Church Assembly. In most dioceses it has not been brought before the clergy as a whole, and the rank and file of church people, upon whom these decisions fall, have had no opportunity of expressing their assent or dissent. Meanwhile in many people there is a deep sense of the hardship that is inflicted by these regulations upon the really innocent party in a divorce suit, and upon the person whom he or she may wish to marry, and many parochial clergy feel keenly the unhappy position into which it brings them with some of their best parishioners. Indeed, some have declared their unwillingness to be bound by these regulations. With most people, however, their dissatisfaction is largely inarticulate, for they find it difficult to give formal expression to their point of view in such a way as to dispute the apparently dogmatic logic of those who take the rigorist[1] view. Indeed, the rigorists tend to regard any other point of view than their own as that of leniency and expediency, based on no defensible theological position.

The first part of this book is an attempt to challenge this assumption, and to show that opposition to the rigorist position can be based upon logical reasoning and the essential principles of Christ's moral teaching and example.

The second part of the book considers this diversity of opinion and practice to which we have referred, and seeks to examine again the sources of authority to which they all look, namely, the words of Christ as recorded in the Gospels and the practice of the Church. We shall find in this re-examination that assumptions have been based on Christ's words which they cannot carry, and that the marked difference in practice between the Eastern Church and the Western Church (after the twelfth century) is due to the rise of this mistaken interpretation of Christ's teaching. If this can be established, it will greatly relieve the tension of conflicting views in the mind of many Christian people, and also provide a bridge between Christian and non-Christian social reformers.

In the light of the conclusions reached a suggestion is put forward of an alternative line of action by the Church, which would bring her whole influence to bear at the point where the problem is actually being faced between husband and wife, before divorce proceedings are contemplated. This would be far more effective to the solution of this problem than the present prohibitive and disciplinary proposals.

[1] The word 'rigorist' is used throughout as a convenient term by which to denote those who believe that Our Lord's words about marriage must be strictly applied, in the sense in which they understand them. It carries no further implication.

Finally, an attempt is made to consider the deep spiritual significance of Christ's teaching about marriage, and to relate it to the situation in which we find ourselves today.

The title of the book may to some people sound provocative, but, after all, Christ Himself used the same expression in regard to one of the most ancient and unquestioned ordinances of God, the Sabbath. In doing this He in no way belittled the Sabbath, but rather exalted it from the position of being a taboo, and revealed it as a divine institution containing a deep purpose for mankind, which would only be obscured and denied by a rigid external observance that contravened man's instinctive moral standards. On the other hand, to say that the Sabbath was made for man did not imply that it was left to man's judgement to make what he liked of the Sabbath. Rather, it gave the Sabbath a deep importance for every man, as containing a divine purpose, which he should seek to discover and fulfil, and which he could only disregard to his own hurt.

In the same way, the application of this concept to marriage implies that the purpose for mankind, involved in the divine intent that marriage should be a permanent, lifelong relationship between one man and one woman, can never be achieved by a rigid, external discipline that offends the moral instincts of innocent people. At the same time, it does not imply that the permanence of the relationship is to be left to the individual judgement of the persons concerned. On the contrary, it states to all who marry that there is a divine intent in the permanence of their relationship, that they can disregard only to their own deep loss.

II

The Present Position

*

The Act of Convocation in which the Convocation of Canterbury has set out its Regulations concerning Marriage and Divorce is printed in full on p. 13 ff. The Regulations can be summed up as twofold: a refusal to allow such a remarriage in church as long as the former partner of either is alive; and a requirement that the admission to Holy Communion of those so remarried by civil law is to be controlled by the discretion of the diocesan bishop.

In promulging this formal Act of Convocation in October, 1957, the Archbishop of Canterbury used these words. 'This Act has no statutory force and is not a law, though it has that spiritual force which properly belongs to the Church's highest instrument of spiritual authority. Clergymen who disobey it do so at their own spiritual peril.'

Later the Archbishop withdrew the words 'spiritual peril', because to some clergymen they carried a condemnatory meaning, beyond the spiritual warning which he had meant to express in using them. He went on: 'At an earlier stage of Canon Law revision, it was proposed that the Church should include in one of the revised Canons a clause to make it an offence to marry such people, and to seek for it statutory authority. That would be to take away the freedom which still remains by the law of the land and of which some few clergy choose to avail themselves in spite of the regulations of Convocation. Convocation decided not to take this action for reasons which I stated at length here in full Synod on 17 May, 1956.'

These references to the dissenting clergymen must be compared with the earlier words to which the Archbishop referred. They were as follows:

'There are some clergy who value very highly, on matters of conscience, the liberty which still remains to them under the civil law to take the marriage of a person who has been divorced. They justify it by their own reading of Scripture. My experience of them is that they are deeply concerned for the freedom of their conscience, which they value very highly indeed. Whenever you get people fighting on the ground of conscience, my own experience of life is that the wisest thing to do is to leave them their freedom.'

Clearly, if people are deliberately left their liberty in order that they may not be prevented from obeying their deeply held conscientious convictions, they cannot be regarded as rebellious or disloyal for doing so. At a later stage we shall consider more fully this question of the authority of Convocation, but one may compare at once another authoritative pronouncement about it, only twenty-two years ago, in June, 1935, in the Upper House of Canterbury Convocation, by Archbishop Lang, whose strictness of view and breadth of statesmanship no one can call in question. He was replying to a protest the previous day by Bishop Furse, the Bishop of St Albans. He and Bishop Heywood of Ely had found themselves in a minority of two, on their proposal to excommunicate all persons who were married while the former partner of either of them was still alive. They could see that they would be overwhelmingly defeated by a vote of the Upper House. At this point Bishop Furse spoke as follows:

'There was a definite way of legislating for the Church, and that was by canon, but it had become rather a habit of late to think that because the House of Bishops or the House of Clergy—but especially the House of Bishops—voted and passed a resolution, the Bishops and Clergy were therefore bound by it. He admitted it was a very nice moral question as to how far they were morally bound by such Resolutions, and he for one should hope to give very grave consideration to that question from a moral point of view, but he must absolutely protest that he was not bound in law by any mere Resolution passed by the Upper House, or passed by the Upper House in conjunction with the Lower House, or endorsed by the House of Laity. He had never yet considered himself and he was not going to consider himself so bound in the future.'

The following day Archbishop Lang replied to this. He dwelt on the question of moral compulsion. 'The position,' he said, 'is simply this. These Resolutions of Convocation are not binding upon members of Convocation, or upon the Church generally, *in the sense that to disregard them would be an act of disloyalty to the Church*, but even in their present form they have a real authority as expressing the mind of Convocation. Those who accept and act upon these Resolutions know that they have this measure of authority behind them; those who decide not to accept and act upon them have the responsibility of setting this measure of authority aside.'

In other words, the authority of Convocation resolutions is the authority of expressed *opinion*—'the *mind* of Convocation'—not the authority of command or direction. To refuse to be bound by them does not involve disloyalty, but it does involve that deep spiritual and moral *responsibility*, which is always present when the conscience of the few differs from that of the majority. That must be faced. In 1935 we have a bishop refusing to be bound by the Resolutions of Convocation, in defence of what he believed to be orthodoxy. Today we have priests making the same refusal, in defence of their legal right to behave in a way which they believe to be Christian and humane. In neither case is their dissent disloyalty.

After all, this is not the first time that this situation has arisen in the Church. Convocation has just formulated a canon permitting a variety of clerical dress at the celebration of Holy Communion. This freedom of use would not exist today had not some clergy in the nineteenth century—and they of the same school of thought as those who now demand a rigid uniformity of action —defied, on conscientious grounds, not only the opinion of the Convocations, but canon law and statute law. So too, did the translators of the Bible in the fifteenth and sixteenth centuries, in defiance of the laws both of Church and State.

The clergy who dissent from the present Act of Convocation do not do so on personal grounds, merely to assert their legal freedom of action. They do so in defence of what they believe to be the spiritual right of those innocently involved in divorce, and because they feel that the present attitude of Convocation is not the right Christian approach to this problem. Our first task must be to consider the grounds on which they hold these convictions.

To deal first with the regulation that the Church will not allow the marriage in church of anyone who has a former partner still living, the first objection to this is that it is universal in application and entirely rejects the clause 'except for fornication' in two passages in St Matthew's Gospel. Indeed, the Archbishop of Canterbury in his book *Problems of Marriage and Divorce*, gives as one of the grounds of the Act of Convocation that 'scholars on their own grounds had ceased to regard the Matthean exception as an authentic "word of our Lord".' This is certainly not the opinion of all scholars, and in the debates in Convocation it was pointed out, both by Bishop Headlam of Gloucester, a former Regius Professor of Divinity at Oxford University, and also by Dr Matthews, Dean of St Paul's, that this was a very insecure and dangerous line for Convocation to take. The rejection of these clauses is only an opinion of Higher Criticism, *based on no textual evidence*, but only upon an assumption of a certain relationship between the synoptic Gospels. The conclusions of Higher Criticism, they pointed out, could equally well be used to throw doubt upon accepted beliefs of the Church.

In point of fact, the very latest New Testament criticism is now beginning to discard the assumption of this relationship between the Gospels. In any case, the fact remains that these clauses of exception have always been part of the accepted canonical text of St Matthew, and no Higher Criticism nor resolution of Convocation can dispute the claim of individual church people to accept them as authoritative words of Christ. In the next chapter we shall find the clearest evidence for doing so.

The second objection is that this regulation makes no distinction between the innocent and guilty parties in a divorce, and inflicts a grievous and deeply-felt hurt upon Christian people who have suffered the wreck of their first marriage through no fault of their own, and are anxious to have the blessing of God upon a new union, which they believe it is God's will that they should enter upon.

This sense of injustice to the innocent party was felt strongly in the earlier debates in Convocation, and it was answered in different ways. One answer was that it is impossible to discover who is the innocent party. Twenty years ago collusion was widespread, but it is now much more controlled, as the onus of proving that there is no collusion is now laid upon the Court. To argue that in many cases there is wrong on both sides and that the conduct of the petitioner may have contributed to the break-up of the marriage is quite irrelevant to the question of remarriage or admission to Holy Communion. The innocent party in a divorce is the one whose conduct has not been the ground upon which the divorce has been granted. In any case, it were far better that some unworthy persons should enjoy the privileges of supposed innocence—a responsibility which weighs on them and not on the Church—than that an innocent person should suffer unjustly.

Another answer to this plea is that hard cases make bad law. That is an excellent reply in law, but it is no argument for followers of Christ. It is an argument that could have been used against Christ Himself over and over again by the Pharisees, on the ground of keeping the Sabbath, an ordinance of unquestioned divine authority. Christ always took the side of the real needs of the individual against the harsh application of the general law, as in His appeal to the historic instance of David and the shew-bread. It might well have been urged by the Pharisees that 'in order to maintain the principle' of the Sabbath, healing should not take place on the Sabbath in the Temple or in a synagogue, but it was there that Jesus did his work of healing.

This attitude of Christ, in putting the fundamental needs of the individual before the rigid observance of even a divine law, his statement that divine laws were made for man's benefit, and that man was not made to be an unvarying example of the strict enforcement of the law; the manifest way in which his compassion for the individual was his governing motive even in the most unequivocal legal situation; all this is the *unique* element in Christ's teaching and practice, that can never be made second to the rigid enforcement even of his own pronouncements.

The Resolution of Convocation, that 'in order to maintain the principle of lifelong obligation which is inherent in every legally contracted marriage', the Church should not allow the marriage in church of *any* divorced person, seems to be quite contrary to Christ's example. It is putting loyalty to the letter of the law above the deep personal need of a human being. It does not take much imagination to realize the feelings of a Christian woman, whose honestly undertaken marriage has been wrecked by a worthless man, and who, perhaps after years of sorrow and disillusionment, wins the love of a good man, to find that marriage to him is regarded as a violation of Christ's law and that she is debarred from receiving the full blessing of God upon this love that has brought her new hope. With no sense of guilt, she feels herself under an undeserved stigma, and, even worse, one that extends to the man she loves.

It is no valid argument to say that the number of innocent persons who desire remarriage in church is few, for Christ continually taught that in the sight of God the need of the individual is as important as that of the crowd. In point of fact the number of innocent parties who would desire to be remarried in church, if the ban of Convocation were removed, is clearly very large.

Finally, it is urged that the vows which are made before God in the marriage service—of lifelong attachment to one another 'till death us do part'—make it sacrilege and perjury to take the same vows to another person while a former partner is still alive. It is sometimes added that the promises were made 'for better or for worse', and that that covers all contingencies.

The argument sounds at first very cogent, but it will not bear examination. In the first place the words 'for better or for worse', refer to the bettering or worsening of the person's condition by the marriage, either in social position or in general good fortune. They cannot possibly mean 'whether you are consistently unfaithful, or persistently cruel, or completely desert me'. No bridegroom or bride could ever have such a meaning of these words in his or her mind. Moreover, they would make nonsense of the promise made 'to love and to cherish'.

The vow made, however, is so binding that it cannot be dissolved by the will of the persons who made it. That is recognized by the law of the land. But if a competent authority, whether of Church or State, which recognizes the lifelong, God-ordained nature of the marriage vow, declares, on the petition of either party, that

events have arisen which make impossible the conditions
implicit in the vows, and on that ground itself annuls
the contract, then the parties are no longer bound by
their previous vows, any more than they would be bound
by any other binding contract, which a competent
authority had abrogated. The vows have been annulled
and they are clearly free to make similar vows to another
person without any stigma of perjury.

To turn now to the second part of the Convocation
regulations—that all remarried divorced persons and
those to whom they are married can only be admitted—
or readmitted—to Holy Communion by the written permission of the diocesan bishop—those who dissent from
this do so on several grounds.

In the first place, although the regulation of Convocation tempers discipline with pastoral mercy, it clearly
implies that, without the bishop's permission, those who
have remarried while a former partner of either is alive
are thereby debarred from receiving Holy Communion.
All who have been confirmed have the right to receive
Holy Communion, and the bishop's order that these persons are to be admitted to Holy Communion only by
his permission must imply that they have been, by their
remarriage, excluded from it. The Lambeth Conference,
in 1888 and again in 1908, refused to recommend such
a discipline, passing this resolution:

'That recognizing the fact that there has always been
a difference of opinion in the Church on the question
whether our Lord meant to forbid marriage to the
innocent party in a divorce for adultery, the Conference recommends that the clergy should not be instructed to refuse the sacraments or other privileges

of the Church to those who, under civil sanction, are thus married.'

Holy Communion is declared by the Church to be 'generally necessary to salvation', and only those are to be repelled from it who are 'notorious and open evil-livers'. To use it as a discipline against people for doing, with the full approval of their own conscience, what is permitted and regularly practised in the Orthodox Church, the Church of Scotland, and other Christian Churches, and is approved by a considerable number of the clergy and a large proportion of the laity of the Church of England, appears to many people to be a complete distortion of any spiritual conception of Church discipline. It creates a situation which offends the moral sense, not only of those against whom it is directed, but of very many others, both within and without the Church.

Furthermore, there is a complete illogicality in this regulation. It brings the whole weight of discipline against remarriage after divorce, whereas the real point at which discipline should be applied, if it is to be applied at all, should be divorce itself. There is not a word in the Marriage Service about remarriage after divorce. It is not even considered. All that is pointed out—and it is pointed out most categorically—is that, in accordance with Christ's words, divorce is never lawful. If that is observed, remarriage does not arise.

But the Church tolerates divorce, inasmuch as it imposes no discipline on those who are divorced, whether innocent or guilty. It cannot be argued, in defence of this, that the Church regards a state divorce as only *a mensa et thoro*, that is, as equivalent to a legal separation, for the parties have deliberately had recourse to a legal process whereby each is free to marry another, and, moreover, should a reconciliation be effected between the parties themselves, they cannot live together again as man and wife without being remarried. Divorce is the point at which the strict Christian conception of marriage is violated, and the responsibility for having recourse to the legal abrogation of that ideal rests with the petitioner, that is, the wronged partner! By seeking a divorce instead of a legal separation, he or she has rejected the Prayer Book ideal in the Marriage Service that divorce 'should never be lawful'.

But the Church imposes no discipline on those who divorce their partners; in fact, Convocation has refused to do so on several occasions. It would raise a public outcry should the wronged party be so disciplined, and the guilty party is plainly not responsible for recourse having been made to divorce, as he or she did not present the petition. Thus divorced persons live unrebuked as Churchpeople—except by the Mothers' Union—and are accepted as communicants. But if they seek to remarry, a contingency which is involved in the complete dissolution of their former marriage, against which the Church has taken no action, they find themselves subject to the possibility of exclusion from Holy Communion. It is morally anomalous.

Another objection to this regulation is that while in some cases it may provide a pastoral opportunity, in most cases it tends to alienate the parties concerned from the Church. It might have been effective in days when everyone was a communicant and exclusion was regarded as a matter of extreme spiritual peril. But today, when to be a communicant is the exception rather than the rule, those who *desire* to receive Holy Communion and find themselves subject to repulsion for an action for which their own conscience does not rebuke them, are likely to withdraw from the Church altogether.

Perhaps the anomaly of applying the discipline of excommunication in cases of marriage after divorce, can best be illustrated by the methods suggested for working this discipline by two bishops who have taken the lead in the rigorist attitude towards marriage and divorce, and both of whom have published their views in book form; namely Dr Mortimer, Bishop of Exeter, and the late Dr Kirk, formerly Bishop of Oxford.

Dr Mortimer, in the chapter which he added to his revision of Dr Lacey's book *Marriage in Church and State*, takes a wholly uncompromising attitude. 'The Church', he says, 'must not allow any of her members to take advantage of the permission accorded by the State to the divorced to remarry.' Then he goes on to consider hard cases:

'It sometimes happens that even loyal, well-instructed and devoted Christians do not obey this call. They are convinced in their consciences that for them, in their circumstances, it is right to marry again. The Church is far from regarding these people as "open and notorious evil-livers". She does not condemn them as immoral and irresponsible; on the contrary, she respects the judgment of conscience, even when it is erroneous, and *expects a man to obey it*, though that means that he disobeys her. *Nevertheless, she asks these people not to present themselves at the Altar*. It cannot be said too often or too clearly that the Church does not reproach with personal immorality those who remarry in good faith. *No moral stigma attaches to her exclusion of them from the*

Altar. . . . That this involves a real hardship and priva-
tion cannot be denied. Yet the extent of the hardship
is sometimes exaggerated. . . . Though they may not,
for the sake of others, approach God through Communion, which is for other Christians the normal
means of grace, yet in prayer and meditation, they
may draw near to Him.'[1]

That an Anglo-Catholic bishop should attempt to minimize the spiritual desolation of lifelong exclusion from
Holy Communion, which the Church teaches 'is generally necessary to salvation', of persons whom the Church
does not condemn as immoral, only emphasizes the
dilemma into which this form of discipline leads.

Bishop Kirk, dealing in his book *Marriage and Divorce*
with the same class of persons, points out that they '*must
be adjudged guiltless before God*'. He takes a more lenient
line towards them, but one, in some ways, even more
incomprehensible. He claims that it is right that the
Church should refuse any application for communion in
a parish 'where the facts are known and much scandal is
caused to many faithful people'. Then he continues, 'I
have said nothing about requiring them to abstain from
communicating in places where neither they nor their
circumstances are known. They are in good conscience
before God in this matter; and provided that they take
effective precautions to do nothing which will cause
scandal or embarrassment, I cannot see that any good
purpose would be served by laying this further burden
upon them.'[2] Quite apart from suggesting a line of action
which, in this most sacred act, involves a deliberate

[1] *Marriage in Church and State*, Lacey, pp. 211, 212.
[2] *Marriage and Divorce*, p. 139.

secretiveness, the danger of being recognized and de-
nounced, and a sense of deceit towards the celebrant in
the strange church, these people are to exclude themselves
from their own parish altar, not for any wrong they have
done, but merely to avoid scandalizing their Christian
fellow-worshippers in the parish.

Bishop Kirk explicitly justifies this demand by a reference to St Paul's direction in Rom. xiv. and 1 Cor. viii.
This, however, is a quite unjustifiable interpretation of
St Paul's words. So far from teaching that a man should
avoid an action for which his own conscience does not
condemn him, because another man does not approve of
it, St Paul emphasizes in this very chapter the duty of
not passing judgement on one another's actions. 'Why
dost thou judge thy brother? Why dost thou set at naught
thy brother? For we shall all stand before the judgement-
seat of God.'[1] What St Paul goes on to say is that if your
conscience-clear action induces a brother, whose own
conscience is not clear on this matter, to act against his
own conscience, and so to commit a sin, then you incur
a certain responsibility. You should ask yourself whether
what you have a right to do is worth doing if it involves
this risk to your weak brother. In the case in point it
was a matter of eating food offered to idols—a matter,
as St Paul said, of little importance. 'To make my brother
to offend' does not mean, to do something which offends
him because he feels I ought not to do it, but to do
something which, because he is a weak man, induces him
to act against his own conscience. The fact that the word
'scandalize' has come to have the former instead of the
latter meaning shows how generally the passage has been
misinterpreted, with the disastrous consequence that

[1] Rom. xiv. 10.

censorious objection to other people's actions, which not only St Paul but, even more, Christ Himself condemned, is not only justified, but claims to be protected even at so high a cost to the spiritual life of the conscience-free person.

The regulations laid down by Convocation in regard to admission to Holy Communion are of a much milder nature than those to which I have referred, but they still impose an intolerable humiliation on innocent people. The situation is somewhat blurred by including the desire to be baptized or confirmed with the desire to partake of Holy Communion. Baptism and confirmation require preparation and approval in the case of *any* person, but the desire to receive Holy Communion—provided one has been confirmed—needs no permission. Every confirmed person has a right to this unless they be debarred as 'open and notorious evil-livers'. That the innocent party in a divorce, who has remarried, and who, as Bishop Kirk wrote, 'must be adjudged guiltless before God', should not be admitted to Holy Communion until his or her case—and that of their wife or husband—has been submitted to the bishop, and granted a written approval, is an interference with individual conscience, and will certainly prove unworkable. Perhaps the most amazing part of this resolution is its conclusion.

> 'This approval shall be given in writing and shall be accepted as authoritative both in the particular Diocese and in all other Dioceses of the province.'

What does this mean? Is there to be kept a list of all 'pardoned divorcees' which is supplied to the bishops? Or has the person concerned to register himself or herself, on arrival in a new diocese, as a 'divorcee re-admitted to Holy Communion' and produce the written permit? Or is it the duty of his or her former incumbent to pass this knowledge on to the new incumbent, who then passes it on to the bishop? Is the fact of the break-down of their former marriage to be proclaimed wher-ever they go? If it is a woman, some watchful member of the Mothers' Union may discover that she has been divorced. Will she then have the right to ask the incumbent if the newcomer has an episcopal permit? The whole thing would be ridiculous, if it were not so humiliating and distressing to those on whom it might be imposed. It is to be hoped that the laity, who are having this discipline imposed upon them without any consultation, will refuse to submit to it. They have the law on their side.

What is surely needed, instead of this complicated and anomalous discipline, is that the Church should point out to all Christian people that there are cases of re-marriage after divorce in which God Himself imputes no guilt, as Bishop Kirk reminds us, and that we must not pass judgement upon one another in the matter. As a matter of fact, most of the communicants in a parish would resent the exclusion from Communion of one of their number merely because he or she had re-married after divorce, nor could even the former partner feel that a wrong was committed against him or her by their presence at Holy Communion, inasmuch as they had, of their own free will, secured the dissolution of the relationship between them.

Apart, however, from the anomalous working of this discipline, and the morally incongruous situations in which even its strongest advocates are involved in the application of it, there is one compelling objection to it—*that it is wholly illegal.* This is set out quite clearly by Bishop Kirk. 'The Church has no longer any legal right to impose the discipline of excommunication upon the laity in this matter; and any bishop or priest who attempted to do so would be severely censured by the judge, if the case ever came into court, on the ground that the remarriage of divorced persons is expressly permitted by the law of the land, and therefore cannot be treated as a moral offence.'[1]

But the illegality goes further still. The whole process of establishing discipline by Convocation resolutions is itself illegal. Canonical legislation in the Church of England since the Reformation is governed by the Act for the Submission of the Clergy. The relevant clauses may be summarized as follows:

1. That the clergy can assemble in Convocation only by authority of the King's writ.

2. That they can draw up constitutions, ordinances, or canons, only with the King's assent and licence.

3. That such canons are inoperative until they receive the royal assent.

4. That even then they are inoperative if they offend against the royal prerogative or the law and custom of the land.

5. That any attempt to establish or 'put into use' any such canons or ordinances, 'by whatsoever name or names they may be called in their Convocations in time coming', except in the prescribed canonical form shall be punishable by imprisonment or fine.[2]

---

[1] *Marriage and Divorce*, p. 138.

[2] *The Canon Law of the Church of England*—Report of the Archbishops' Commission on Canon Law, 1947, p. 71.

It is to be noted that this Act does not only enact that the Convocations can make canons only with the licence of the Crown, and that the canons are inoperative unless and until they receive the Royal assent, and, even then, if and so far as they offend against the royal prerogative or the law or custom of this country. The Act does more than this. It *forbids* the clergy in Convocation, under threat of severe penalties, to enact, promulge or execute any such canons, constitutions or ordinance provincial, '*by whatsoever name or names they may be called in their Convocations in time coming*', except under these conditions. In other words, no order nor regulations can be laid down by Convocation even under the name of an Act of Convocation, nor any attempt made to 'put them into use', *except as canons, under the prescribed conditions*.

It might have been argued in 1936 that, Canon Law having been for so long almost in abeyance, the Church had no way of dealing with the problem of marriage and divorce, except by expressing her corporate *opinion* in Convocation resolutions. Now, however, that the Convocations have applied for and received the Royal licence to promulge canons embodying the Church's constitutions and ordinances, in the manner legally prescribed and are engaged in drafting them, the situation is entirely different. In their canonical proposals the Convocations drafted the first of the two new regulations as a clause in a canon, in the following words:

'No Minister shall solemnize matrimony, or allow matrimony to be solemnized in the church or chapel of which he is the Minister, between two persons either of whom is a person who has already been married but whose marriage has been dissolved by secular authority, so long as the husband or wife to whom the person was married is still living.'

There was a plain intention here of abolishing by Canon Law the existing freedom of the clergy. In May, 1956, on the recommendation of the Standing Committee, Convocation withdrew the clause from the canon. What is most significant is the grounds upon which it was considered that the clause should be withdrawn. In conveying to the Upper House of Canterbury this recommendation the Archbishop of Canterbury said:

'To include an expression of this kind in a canon would require a change of statute law, for all that the present law does is to give the minister the right to marry a divorced person in church while a former partner is still living, the final responsibility for decision being left to him.

'We can take for granted that Parliament will scrutinize very carefully any canon which appears to limit the liberty at present enjoyed by citizens or clergy. There are some clergy who value very highly, on matters of conscience, the liberty which still remains to them under the civil law to take the marriage of a person who has been divorced. They justify it by their own reading of Scripture. They will take every step to make sure they are not deprived of this liberty. They will have the instinctive sympathy of a very large number of members of Parliament. A number of the laity of the Church of England would also like that liberty to be retained.

'If that be the state of opinion in general, *it would seem unwise to seek battle with Parliament* on that particular ground of trying to get a limitation of a freedom which some people intensely value and which many people generally favour.'

It should be noted that the threat to existing liberty in the draft clause is not only to the liberty of the clergy, but also to that of the laity. Under the existing law the innocent party in a divorce has the right to be married in church if the incumbent is willing. To forbid all clergymen to take such a marriage takes away this liberty of the laity.

The decision to omit this clause from the canon was passed almost unanimously in the Upper Houses of both Convocations. When this decision was conveyed to the Lower House of Canterbury Convocation, it was pointed out that this did not imply that the Church was moving from the position which she had taken up, but that she would rely upon the authority of the Resolutions of Convocation. One of the bishops present immediately pointed out that the Church cannot have two sources of binding authority. Having decided to embody her rules and regulations in canons, she cannot claim authority for Convocation resolutions. This is particularly so in regard to this clause. For, having deliberately refused to embody it in a canon on three grounds; that it contravenes a law which the State will be unwilling to alter; that it arouses the conscientious objection of a number of clergy, a considerable proportion of Church laity, a majority of Members of Parliament, and a very large number of citizens generally; and that it has no likelihood of securing the Royal Assent; Convocation has now embodied this clause, together with other regulations and disciplines, in its own resolutions, and, under the name of 'An Act of Convocation', is attempting to 'put them in use' by every means short of the legal compulsion which it knows it cannot secure. It is a clear contravention of the Act of Henry VIII.

It is quite obvious that at the Reformation it was determined that the Church of England should no longer be a hierarchy like the Church of Rome; that it should not be governed solely by the bishops and clergy acting in Convocation, but that their rule should be controlled by the Royal Assent and the existing law of the land. This was enforced by the threat of legal penalties should ever any attempt be made by Convocation to put forward regulations on its sole authority. The recognition of this Act of Convocation as something which 'ought to be obeyed' involves the abandonment of this principle which was fundamental to the Reformation and a disregard of the law of the land in regard to ecclesiastical government. Still less can there be any weight in the directions of individual bishops to the clergy of their diocese to obey these Resolutions. The bishops have no power to issue directions on their own authority, nor on the authority of an Act of Convocation which is not a canon. The clergy promise canonical obedience in things lawful and honest. Any assumption of episcopal authority that goes beyond that is contrary to the whole spirit of the Church of England and involves a conception of episcopacy which would be a complete barrier to reunion with the non-episcopal Churches.

On all these grounds it is hard to see how those who cannot feel bound by these regulations of Convocation can be regarded as disloyal or rebellious. Their dissent, however, does not imply that they think that the Church should acquiesce in the present position in regard to divorce, and take no action to establish and strengthen the Christian principle of lifelong marriage. There remains another way, and that is to consider again whether the scriptural and ecclesiastical grounds permit of a less rigorous attitude to the problem, and whether a form of pastoral guidance could be evolved that would carry with it a wider moral approval.

III

What Christ Said and What the Church Did

A. THE NEW TESTAMENT

The whole attitude of the Christian Church towards marriage is dependent upon the teaching of Christ as recorded in the Gospels. It can be summed up in the two sayings which, in the English translation, are so inclusive and categorical as to appear to leave no room for misinterpretation.

'What God hath joined together, let not man put asunder',

and

'Whosoever putteth away his wife and marrieth another, committeth adultery; and he that marrieth her that is put away from her husband, committeth adultery.'

These words, as they stand, are the basis of the rigorist attitude to this problem, and even those who feel that Christ was stating an ideal and not laying down binding regulations, cannot but wonder why He phrased the ideal in such a categorical and conclusive way.

Moreover, it is hard to understand how St Paul, when

the Church was hardly twenty years old, felt able to authorize exceptions to so unequivocal a commandment. Again, it is hard to understand how the Early Church, in varying degrees, sanctioned a departure from this explicit rigid standard, how the Justinian Code of the sixth century could fix such relaxation in a legal enactment, and how the Eastern Orthodox Church has always accepted that position.

The answer to this perplexity is to be found in the fact that, if we turn again to the Greek original of the Gospels, we discover that in regard to the key saying, 'What God hath joined together, let not man put asunder', *the English is not a correct translation of the Greek, nor was it so understood in the Early Church.*

To make this clear to the ordinary reader necessitates an explanation of Greek usage that is familiar to any Greek scholar. In the Greek language the only article used is the definite article 'the'. Where a noun is used without the article, the meaning is the same as in the use in English of the indefinite article, 'a'. Thus in Greek you have 'man' as equivalent to the English 'a man'.

Again, in English, the *collective* word 'man', implying 'mankind in general', is expressed by omitting the article altogether. In Greek it is expressed by the *use* of the definite article. Thus, in Greek 'the man' either refers to a specific individual denoted by the context, or it means 'mankind'. Now, in both the passages in the New Testament in which this saying of Christ occurs (Matt. xix. 6 and Mark x. 9) *there is no definite article before the word 'man'*, and this is all the more emphatic because in both passages the definite article is used with 'God', as signifying the supreme Divine Being and not just 'a god'. The word *anthropos* stands without the article, and

43

can only mean 'a man'. Therefore, what Jesus said was:
'What God hath joined together, a man must not put
asunder.'[1]

But there is still more in the significance of this saying.
The Greek word for 'man' (*anthropos*) signified 'a human
being', though it was more often used of the male sex.
'A certain man [*anthropos*] went down from Jerusalem to
Jericho' (Luke x. 30). It was not normally used to mean
'husband', which was expressed by the Greek word
aneer, in contradistinction to *gyné* ('woman' or 'wife').

Just, however, as we speak in English of 'man and
wife', using the generic word 'man' in the meaning of
'husband', so it was possible to use the Greek word
anthropos. This was an uncommon use, but in point of
fact Christ used the word *anthropos* in this sense *in the
previous verse*, when He quoted from Gen. ii. 24: 'For this
cause shall a man (*anthropos*) leave his father and mother
and cleave to his wife (*gyné*).' This is not a disputable
Greek translation of our Lord's words, spoken origin-
ally in Aramaic. It is an exact quotation from the Septuagint, the official Greek version of the Hebrew Scriptures,
compiled three centuries before Christ. In this passage
Christ bases His pronouncement upon the word of God
which He quotes from Genesis, and the immediate re-
petition of the word *anthropos*, just as it stands in that
passage, and the emphatic position in which it is placed,
indicate clearly that the meaning of the word is the same
in both places. This double use of *anthropos* in this un-
usual sense by the Evangelist must be taken as giving

[1] Throughout the Gospels *anthropos* without the article always means
'a man'. There are two or three passages in the Epistle to the Hebrews
(ii. 6, viii. 2, xiii. 6) and in 1 Cor. xv. 21, where it occurs and is rendered
in the English translation 'man'. In every case it cannot mean 'mankind',
and should be translated 'a man'. In English 'man' is often used to mean
'a human being'.

the exact meaning of the original Aramaic in which it was spoken.

'For this cause shall *anthropos* leave his father and mother and cleave to his wife and the twain shall become one flesh. . . . What God hath joined together, *anthropos* cannot put asunder.'

Finally, a few verses later (Matt. xix. 10) the disciples also use the same word *anthropos* to denote 'a married man', and here they use it with the definite article, in the collective sense of 'man and wife'. 'If this is the relationship of man and wife [*the anthropos* and *the gyné*] it is better not to marry.'

Thus we have the word *anthropos* used three times in the sense of 'a married man' or 'husband' in six consecutive verses (Matt. xix. 6-10) in the passage describing this incident. The natural, and indeed the grammatical, translation of Christ's words is: 'What therefore God hath joined together a man [in this context 'a married man', 'a husband'] must not put asunder.'

In order fully to grasp the significance of this pronouncement by Christ, we must consider the attitude towards marriage and divorce in Jewish law. Under Roman law marriage was a private contract between a man and a woman, which could be brought to an end by either party and, although the Lex Julia of 18 B.C. had introduced penalties against the abuse of divorce, in the Roman Empire marriage was still regarded as a private contract. But in Judaism marriage was a tribal matter, carefully controlled, and inwrought into the religious and social pattern of the Jewish race. One of the central religious concerns of Judaism was the purity of the race and of its individual families, and the continuance of the succession of each generation. Unchastity was a sin against the family and the race, and was dealt with by legal enactment, and the begetting of children was a duty which no one could avoid. If after ten years a wife was still barren, unless her husband already had two children by a former marriage, he was compelled by the Law to put her away and marry another woman.

Marriage legislation in the early written law, which we find in Leviticus, Numbers and Deuteronomy, was comparatively simple. Adultery was punished by the death of the adulteress and her paramour, and in the case of suspected adultery there was a solemn testing of the wife's innocence by a ritual before the priest, known as 'the drinking of the bitter water' (Num. v. 11-31). Even the premarital unchastity of a wife, if discovered, was punishable by death (Deut. xxii. 20).

There was also in the early written law a permission for divorce, and as this permission was the root of the whole dispute about divorce amongst the Jews of our Lord's time and also the background to His own pronouncements, it is important to consider it carefully. This permission is given in Deut. xxiv. 1, and reads as follows:

'When a man taketh a wife and marrieth her, then it shall be, if she find no favour in his eyes, because he hath found some unseemly thing in her, that he shall write her a bill of divorcement, and give it in her hand, and send her out of his house. And when she is departed out of his house, she may go and be another man's wife.'

The word 'unseemly' can either mean 'misshapen' or 'ugly', in which case it would refer to a physical defect;

46

or it can mean 'unseemly' or 'indecorous', which have a moral implication. Quite clearly it cannot in this permission have implied any unchastity, marital or premarital. As we have seen, the punishment for this was death, whereas, under this permission, the divorced wife carried no stigma and could marry another man. It is far more likely that it referred to physical defects or blemishes. There was special concern in Jewish law for the physical purity of the race. Certain bodily defects rendered a man unfit for the priesthood and a woman unfit for marriage, and certain major physical defects in a husband compelled him to release his wife by a bill of divorcement.

When his questioners put forward this Mosaic permission, Christ declared that it had been given 'for the hardness of your hearts'. This could not mean the husband's desire for divorce, for, when the Mosaic permission was given, polygamy was practised among the Hebrews, and an undesired wife was merely another servant. What he seems to refer to was the harshness, the cruelty, of men's hearts. In those days there was little direct physical or mental acquaintance with a wife before marriage, and it might well be that on 'taking her into his own house' some disfigurement might be discovered, creating a physical or mental aversion. In that case the Mosaic direction was that a man should at once give his wife a bill of divorcement, leaving her free to marry another man. It was the protection of an unloved wife from an unhappy life in an age of polygamy. In Deut. xxi. 15ff. there is other legislation to protect the rights of a 'hated' wife and her children.

Now in Judaism it was held that, in addition to the written law, an oral law was given on Mt. Sinai, which was handed on from teacher to disciple, and which carried the same divine authority as the written law. Moreover, this oral law was not a closed system, but was constantly developed in its application to the more settled and increasingly complex life of the nation, on the basis of the written law. This oral law was set out in written form towards the end of the second century A.D. under the title of 'The Mishnah'. It covers four centuries of Jewish religious and cultural activity in Palestine, from about 200 B.C. to A.D. 200. It thus gives a detailed and authoritative account of the Jewish legal background of Our Lord's day.[1]

In the historic evolution of Jewish law, two main changes took place in regard to marriage legislation. In the first place, the strict rule of the death penalty for adultery became modified, though, from the incident in St John's Gospel, it appears to have still applied to cases where the offenders were caught *in flagrante delicto*. But for most cases the Mosaic bill of divorcement had been substituted for the death penalty, not as a permission dependent solely upon the will of the husband, but as a permissive or compulsory direction, laid down by the law in varying circumstances of the proof or presumption of guilt. This covered, not only actual adultery, but loose behaviour which might presume infidelity, which was expressed by the Greek word πορνεια (unchastity).

It must not be imagined that this marriage legislation was entirely in favour of the husband. There were several circumstances under which a wife could claim from her husband a bill of divorcement. For example, normal marital relationships were regarded as essential to marriage, and a continued refusal of such relations by either

[1] See *The Mishnah*, Herbert Danby, O.U.P. (Introduction).

party was a ground of compulsory divorce. Even the right of a husband to divorce his wife for discovered physical defects, was forbidden in the case of visible defects of which he could have been aware before betrothal; and even defects concealed by the clothing were not held to be a valid ground of divorce, where the husband had had opportunity for previous discovery through his own women folk. The rights of women were never more safeguarded in any marriage legislation, except the constitutions of Justinian, until the present century.

This whole complex legal system into which the Mosaic bill of divorcement had been inserted, was regarded, not as man-made, but as having divine authority, and Christ could not have swept it away with one word, without bringing chaos into the religious, social, and ritual life of the nation. The original death sentence for adultery expressed the Jewish view that this crime destroyed the marriage union, and though custom had mitigated this extreme severity, the husband was *compelled* by law to divorce, not only a wife convicted of adultery, but one who, by her own wilful act, had put herself into a situation with her suspected lover, in which adultery could be presumed. Even if Christ's words could be translated 'Whom God hath joined together let not mankind put asunder', they would not have been taken by his hearers as negating this Jewish law of divorce for unchastity which was regarded as having divine authority.

In point of fact, however, Our Lord's questioners were not asking him whether he approved of divorce as it was incorporated in the Jewish law, but they were considering another line of action which lay outside the statutory legal enactments. About the sixth century B.C.

an important change had taken place in Jewish national life in regard to marriage. Monogamy had supplanted polygamy and had thus ended the freedom from self-restraint which a husband had formerly enjoyed. Gradually a tendency arose to invoke the permission granted by Moses, as a release from the restriction of monogamy. There were in Our Lord's day two main schools of thought, the School of Shammai, which held that the Mosaic permission only now applied where it had been incorporated in the law as a penalty for unchastity; and the School of Hillel which claimed that it still gave the husband the right to divorce his wife without any further legal permission, for any action at all which he himself regarded as 'unseemly'. There was also a third, even more lax, school of thought, which came to be associated with the name of the Rabbi Akiba. It took the words in the original Mosaic permission, 'if she find no favour in his eyes', as justifying divorce in order to secure a more attractive wife. This would have opened the way to the unrestricted divorce by mutual consent established among the Gentiles, for a woman, attracted to another man, could persuade or bribe her husband to divorce her. This division of opinion had not been settled in law, but more and more husbands were claiming the right to act on their own interpretation of the Mosaic permission. This was condemned by the prophet Malachi, 400 years before Christ, as a national sin.[1] In Our Lord's day, owing to Gentile influence, it had become a burning issue.

It was this question which was brought to Jesus, and the omission by Mark of the specific words, 'for any

[1] Mal. ii. 13-17. The meaning is set out much more clearly in the Septuagint than in the English version, see p. 100.

cause', makes it all the more clear. The question, 'Is it lawful for a man to put away his wife?', could not have meant, 'Is divorce lawful?', for divorce on certain grounds was embodied in the law and concerning that there was no dispute among the Jews. The only dispute was as to how far a man had the right 'to put away' his wife on his own initiative, outside the provisions of the law. That was the question which was brought to Jesus.

When his questioners quoted the Mosaic permission as their justification, Jesus pointed out its original purpose as the protection of an unloved wife from the hardness of men's hearts, but he did not condemn it, as and when it was given. It was a departure from the divine ideal, necessitated by the imperfection of human nature, and therefore it could not be taken as in itself a criterion of the true nature of marriage, implicit in its original institution by the act of God, as given in the Book of Genesis. Christ applied this divine principle to the situation in the words which, as we have already seen, can only be rightly translated:

'What therefore God hath joined together, a man (in this context "a husband") must not put asunder.'

He brushes aside the question as to the grounds on which a husband can put away his wife, by declaring that a husband has no right of himself to dissolve his own marriage.

This explains the dismayed exclamation of some of Our Lord's followers. It was not the indissolubility of marriage—which they could not have inferred from Christ's words—but it was the altered status of the husband, that startled them. 'If this is the situation between man and wife', they exclaimed, 'it is not expedient to marry.' Where the husband had the right of divorce, he was the undoubted master in his house. In the same way, many men in the nineteenth century resented the 'Married Women's Property Act', because it reduced the mastery of the husband. Christ put his absolute veto on what has always been in the East a corrupting force in society, the unrestricted right of the husband to divorce his wife. It made impossible the realization of God's purpose for man and woman in marriage. In a newspaper report, a year or more ago, of a meeting in Egypt to reform the divorce law of that country, a politician was quoted as saying that the unrestricted right of the husband to end his marriage at any time by divorce, as still exists in Islam, was an outrage on society.

Thus we see that Christ did not declare that marriage was indissoluble, but that it was a divinely-sealed lifelong union, which could not be annulled at the will of the husband, one of the parties to the union. In private to his disciples, as St Mark relates, he extended this prohibition also to the wife, who in the Roman world about them exercised the same right.

But Christ did not stop at the mere denial of the right of husband or wife to dissolve their own marriage. He went on to denounce in unmistakable language the extreme laxity of Akiba, which was, indeed, implicit in the complete freedom of action claimed by the School of Hillel; namely, that a man might divorce his wife if another woman had displaced her in his favour.

'Whosoever shall put away his wife, except for fornication, and shall marry another, committeth adultery, and he that marrieth her when she is put away committeth adultery.'

The form in which this saying is expressed is significant. Divorce and remarriage are coupled together as forming one intent, in the sense, 'Whosoever shall put away his wife *in order to* marry another.'[1] This Christ utterly condemned. 'The man', he said, 'who forsakes his wife for another is an adulterer, even if he attempts to legalize it by a bill of divorcement.' In the same way it could be said today of the facilities for divorce in some parts of the world, that they are nothing but legalized adultery. But that was not to say that all remarriage after divorce was forbidden, as, for example, where the bill of divorcement had been incorporated into the legal process against a wife's unchastity,[2] with the legal *compulsion* in most cases to put her away.[3] It would have been shocking to the Jewish insistence upon the integrity of every man's line of descent and his duty 'to be fruitful and multiply', that a man should be condemned for taking steps to divorce an unfaithful wife, and for seeking another in her place.

This point of view would have been taken for granted by a Jewish audience, but Christ sealed it by the words of the exception, recorded twice by St Matthew, 'except for the cause of fornication'. It was almost inevitable that St Matthew should report this exception in a gospel written for the Palestinian Church, in order to avoid a charge, from Jewish readers, of disregard for the law. It was also natural that St Mark—writing for Roman Christians amongst whom no law existed that would demand this explicit exception—might omit it, and rather record Christ's private words to his disciples, in which he extended his condemnation to the right of

---

[1] See *The Gospels*, tr. Ronald Knox. Note on St Matt. xix. 9.
[2] *Sotah*, VI. 1.   [3] Ibid., V. 1.

women to initiate divorce, allowed under Roman law.
Nevertheless, amongst Romans the omission of the words
of exception would not have been taken to imply the
forbidding of divorce and remarriage in the case of un-
faithfulness, for in Roman society to continue to live
with an unfaithful wife was to incur the charge of being
a procurer.

One of the difficulties which confront the Western
interpretation of Christ's words, as declaring the indissolubility of marriage, is the pronouncement by St Paul,
only twenty years later, to the Corinthian Church, in
which he sanctions, in two cases, divorce and remarriage.
But with the right interpretation of Christ's words, St
Paul's decision appears natural and comprehensible. To
the married he gives Christ's explicit direction that a
man should not put away his wife, and that a woman
who had left her husband should not regard herself as
free to marry again. 'But for the rest', says St Paul—
that is, beyond that explicit direction—'I speak, not the
Lord.'[1] Having declared the principle that neither party
to the marriage has the power in their own right to dissolve it, he proceeds to give authoritative permissions
in certain circumstances. Such circumstances were bound
to arise when converts to Christianity were made in a
community in which the right of divorce was in the
hands of husband or wife. St Paul considers the convert,
already married to a non-Christian partner, and he exhorts
him or her to continue lovingly in their marriage. But
if the non-Christian refuses and divorces the Christian,
the latter is free to marry again.[2] Another case which

[1] The English version, 'To the rest', is incomprehensible, for St Paul
goes on as before, giving direction to the married.
[2] 1 Cor. vii. 12-16.

St Paul considers is that of a man who was already divorced, becoming a Christian. His former wife might be married again to another man. In St Paul's own opinion he would be better advised to remain unmarried. 'But and if thou do marry', he adds, 'thou hast not sinned.'[1]

In regard to these pronouncements of St Paul, Bishop Kirk writes: 'This "Pauline privilege" stands on no recognizable basis of principle.' This is a startling statement, but it is certainly true, if Christ's words are taken in their generally accepted meaning, 'Whom God hath joined together, let not man put asunder.' Indeed, in that case, it is hardly credible that St Paul should not have quoted that categorical pronouncement that marriage could never be dissolved, still less that he should have authorized exceptions to it. But if the words of Christ were, 'Whom God hath joined together, a husband (or wife) cannot put asunder', then St Paul's action is consistent and comprehensible. Having quoted that command as the whole of Christ's teaching, he then goes on to give authoritative permission for remarriage after such a divorce in certain circumstances, and he claims in doing this 'to be faithful', that is, consistent with Christ's mind. Surely in this he gives a clear indication of the right Christian approach to this problem.

It appears then, from the New Testament, that while Christ set out, quite explicitly, that neither partner in a marriage had the right, of their own will, to dissolve it,

[1] 1 Cor. vii. 28. These words are sometimes taken merely as a general permission to marry, but St Paul has already pronounced on that at the beginning of the chapter. In this passage he is treating the problem arising from the pre-Christian circumstances of his converts. The grammatical form of the sentence links it with the preceding verse. The other words in the verse, 'and if a virgin marry she hath not sinned', probably refer to a woman who had taken a vow of virginity under her former religion.

he did not declare that in no circumstances could a marriage be dissolved, or remarriage be permissible. We have in the New Testament four instances in which divorce and remarriage were approved; in the old Mosaic permission in its original circumstances and intention; in the case of an unchaste wife in accordance with Jewish law; and, in Gentile Christianity, in the case of a Christian divorced by a non-Christian partner, or an already divorced man, who had become a Christian.

B. THE EASTERN CHURCH

In considering the attitude of the Early Church to Christ's teaching on marriage and divorce, far greater attention is usually paid to the tradition of the Western, than to that of the Eastern Church, and the recognition by the Eastern Church of the right of Christians, under certain conditions, to the right of divorce and remarriage is generally treated as a departure from the true Christian ideal, due to the weak complaisance of the Eastern Church, in face of what is represented as the secular legislation of Justinian in the sixth century. This is a quite inaccurate presentation of the historical facts, and it is impossible to brush aside in this way the different attitude to this problem in Eastern Christendom to that adopted later in the West.

In the first centuries of Christendom Gentile Christianity was faced by a very difficult problem. While they understood Christ's words in their true sense, not as a declaration of the absolute indissolubility of marriage, but as the prohibition of divorce on the sole authority of the husband or wife, they found themselves in a society in which there was not, as there was in Palestine, any other legal procedure. Clearly, remarriage after such a divorce was contrary to Christ's teaching. Nevertheless, a way out had to be found, and it was found along the lines of St Paul's procedure, in episcopal dispensations. While divorce for adultery, and even on other grounds, was generally permitted, remarriage after such a divorce was only allowed for Christians by episcopal dispensations, which were based upon a general acceptance of the Matthean exception.

Some bishops took a more lenient attitude than others, and consequently provoked a reaction of strictness. It is natural that Councils and canons should be more concerned with restrictions than with episcopal permissions. Even Origen, whose antipathy to sex was expressed in the self-mutilation, which he afterwards repented, agreed that dispensations for remarriage were necessary 'in spite of the express prohibition of Scripture, if regard be paid to the infirmity of men not endowed with the grace of continence, and the worse evils that a strict observance of the law might engender.'[1]

That this attitude to the Matthean exception also existed in the Western Church in the early centuries is plain from the complaint of St Augustine, in the fourth century, that 'the question whether he that putteth away his wife for adultery and marries again is, on that score, an adulterer, is not clear in the divine sayings, and that a man may be supposed to err venially in the matter'. As we shall see, this point of view altered later in the West. In the Eastern Church, however, the acceptance of the Matthean exception, governed by episcopal dispensations, and later by Byzantine law, has always remained.

In the fourth century Christianity became the state religion of the Empire, and with the foundation of the

[1] Origen, *Commentary on St Matthew*, Vol. XIV, p. 23.

new capital at Byzantium and the subsequent division of the Empire into Eastern and Western, the Eastern Church developed within an ordered and civilized community, while the Western Church existed for centuries in the turbulent disorder of a continual succession of barbarian invasions. Moreover, the Eastern Church was more speculative and mystically intellectual than the Western Church, and the foundation of Christian theology in the Ecumenical Councils owes far more to Eastern than to Western thinkers.

'From the end of the fourth century to the middle of the fifteenth, the Byzantine Empire was the centre of a civilization equal to that of any age in brilliance, certainly the most brilliant known to the Middle Ages, and possibly the only real civilization which prevailed in Europe between the close of the fifth century and the beginning of the eleventh.'[1] Moreover, the Byzantine Empire was in its open profession a Christian State. No pagan worship was allowed in the city of Constantinople, and the Patriarch of Constantinople ranked next to the Emperor.

From the fourth century the first Christian Emperors immediately began to codify regulations about marriage and divorce, and to adjust them to Christian principles, but it was not until the Code of Justinian in the sixth century that this was brought into a permanent legal form. This Code was in no way a case of a secular authority presenting the Church with a *fait accompli*, as it is sometimes represented to be. To quote a modern historian: 'The Code of Justinian was drawn up for an Empire that was unequivocally and even aggressively Christian according to its lights. The first title of the

[1] Professor C. Diehl in *Cambridge Mediaeval History*, IV, p. 745.

first book runs, "Of the most High Trinity and the Catholic Faith, and that no one dare publicly to dispute it".[1] Justinian was an ecclesiastically-minded man who believed that the only way to peace and security was uniformity.

The Code itself was a codification and interpretation of the existing laws of the Roman Empire, to which were added 'The Novels', 160 new laws issued by Justinian himself. The justification of this new legislation was based upon a principle of historical evolution that is all too often forgotten, and is very relevant to the problem we are here considering. 'The fact that human nature is constantly changing (as has been said frequently in previous prefaces and will be frequently repeated hereafter as long as nature goes her way) leads us to constant new enactments.'

The enactments deal with three main themes:

(1) civil and military administration;
(2) ecclesiastical and theological matters;
(3) the family and private property.

With their legislation against bribery and corruption, the regulation of state services, the protection of the individual citizen against the tyranny or undue interference of bureaucratic officials, the expedition and fairness of judicial procedure, the legitimizing of illegitimate children, the control of moneylenders and of profiteering, the protection of women from being forced into immorality, the severe punishment of pimps and procurers, the prohibition of the private manufacture of arms and the control of private building in the interests of the community, these 'Novels' indicate a political and civic standard that was not reached

[1] *Justinian and His Age*, P. N. Ure, p. 144.

in the West until the twentieth century. The ecclesiastical regulations themselves aimed at a high level of moral and spiritual efficiency in the ministry, and the control, both of episcopal tyranny or corruption, and of the undue interference of the State in purely ecclesiastical matters.

One of the tasks to which the new legislation had to address itself was, on the one hand, to put an end to the diversity and uncertainty of episcopal dispensations in regard to the right of Christians to remarry after divorce, and, on the other hand, to control the long-existing freedom, under Roman law, of the husband or wife in instituting divorce. It recognized the Christian ideal that the marriage bond was for life and could not be dissolved by the sole action of husband or wife, and it entirely prohibited divorce by mutual consent. It fixed, however, certain grounds for divorce, which constituted the legal authority under which the individual could act. These were, adultery or the attempt to murder husband or wife; the impotence of either party; their absence as a prisoner or a captive for five years; or their being sentenced to penal servitude in the mines. A wife might also be divorced if she committed abortion; went with strangers to disreputable banquets; stayed away from her home without her husband's leave, or went to indecent places of amusement against his wishes. A husband might also be divorced if he attempted to make his wife a prostitute, or if he falsely accused her of adultery in public. Several of these grounds of divorce are identical with those enacted in Jewish law, which would seem to imply that they had already been recognized in episcopal dispensations. The practice of the pagan world itself was checked by an enactment that, if parties divorced one another for reasons which the law did not allow, then both were to be sent to monasteries and their property divided between these monasteries and their heirs.

This constituted strict and uniform divorce legislation for the whole Empire, and it was accepted by the Church as the properly legalized expression of the Christian view that husband and wife had no power of divorce, except on grounds regulated by Christian authority. When a canon of the Quinisext Council, a century and a half later, reiterated the canonical rule that attempted marriage after divorce was adultery, this was not in opposition to Justinian's Code. It was a reassertion of the Christian viewpoint, necessitated by the fact that, on appeal from his non-Christian subjects, Justinian's successor had revoked his restrictions on the free exercise of their right of divorce by non-Christians. The canon laid down that this did not apply to Christians. Dr Lacey points out that the Eastern canonists 'interpreted this canon in the light of Justinian's law. They were unanimous in holding it to forbid, as Justinian's law forbade, divorce by mutual consent, or on any other ground than those laid down by the civil law, or apart from judicial process.' Thus, in the Eastern Church, regulated divorce was not regarded as a loophole from an absolute Christian standard, or as a concession to State authority, but as the expression of the Christian standard of marriage in State legislation, taking into account the frailty of human nature.

As with the shrinking boundaries of the Eastern Empire the rule of the Patriarch of Constantinople extended further than that of the Emperor, the administration of marriage discipline passed more and more into the hands of the Church, but it was still the recognized discipline of a Christian State. This gradual change enabled the

Eastern Church, after the Ottoman conquest, to maintain this Byzantine discipline under the Ottoman State and to enjoy the undisputed control of marriage in regard to Christians. With the break-up of the Ottoman Empire and the liberation of the Christian States of Eastern Europe, the Orthodox Church has recovered, in some measure, the sense of its integral unity with the State.

It is sometimes asserted that the Orthodox Church today regrets the attitude towards controlled divorce that it has taken up for fourteen centuries.[1] In regard to this I quote a passage from a letter which I received in 1938 from the late Archbishop Germanos in reply to an inquiry from me on this point. He writes, 'I should like to say that the facility for divorce strengthens the bond of marriage in our country, in so far as the transgressor knows well that there is in the hands of his wife a means to put an end to his infidelities.'

An even stronger expression of the rightness of the Eastern approach to this problem, as compared with that of the West, can be found in the writings of one of the most distinguished theologians and philosophers of the Russian Orthodox Church, Nicholas Berdyaev, whom Archbishop William Temple described as one of the most discerning and original religious thinkers of our day. He writes as follows:

'To prohibit divorce, as the Roman Catholic Church in particular insists on doing, is one of the most cruel things that can be done to human beings, forcing them to live in an atmosphere of falsity, hypocrisy, and tyranny and to profane their most intimate feelings. The reference to the Gospel which is supposed to proclaim the indissolubility of marriage is particularly unconvincing.

[1] *Marriage and Divorce*, Kirk, p. 44.

The Gospel always reveals absolute life, but that absoluteness is a revelation of the Kingdom of God and not an external norm and law. The prohibition of divorce is based upon a legalistic interpretation of Christianity. It is striking how differently Christians interpret the Gospel teaching about sex and marriage and the Gospel teaching about wealth and property. . . . The Gospel injunctions are absolute in both cases.'[1]

C. THE WESTERN CHURCH

It remains to consider how and why, in view of the long-existing attitude of the Eastern Church, the Western Church of Rome took up the view of the absolute indissolubility of a properly celebrated Christian marriage, an indissolubility that could not be overcome even by Papal action, except on grounds of nullity.

In the first place, while the Eastern Church arrived at their ordering of the problems of marriage and divorce in the legislation of a highly-developed and friendly Christian State, in the West the conditions were utterly different. 'The Empire was broken up, Christianity extended to the Northern nations before it was completely organized, and the religious control of life, in regard to marriage as in other respects, had to be worked out in a welter of confusion. . . . The work was chiefly done (from the fifth to the eleventh century) by the continual exercise of a rather indeterminate discipline, enforcing with more or less efficiency the rules and customs of Christianity.'[2] It was the same confusion of dispensations that had been brought to an end in the Eastern Empire in the sixth century by the Code of Justinian,

[1] *The Destiny of Man*, pp. 296, 297.
[2] *Marriage in Church and State*, T. A. Lacey, pp. 112, 113.

but in the West it was not until the twelfth century—
six centuries after the legislation of Justinian had been
established—that the *Decretum* of Gratian collected and
classified the previous decisions. They did not take final
shape in the Body of Canon Law until 1483.

The important distinction in the attitude towards divorce in the codified Canon Law of Western Christendom from the practice of the Eastern Church was its
declaration of the complete indissolubility of a properly
contracted marriage. Not even the Pope could annul a
true marriage. The authority invoked for such a view
was the word of Christ, 'Whom God hath joined together
let not man put asunder.' The obstacle was not, as in
the Eastern Church, the impossibility of man or wife
putting an end to their own marriage, but the absolute
indissolubility of marriage. It is not difficult to see how
in the West this interpretation of Christ's words arose.
After the fourth century, if not earlier, the knowledge
of Greek disappeared from Western Christendom, and
the Bible was known only in the Latin version, the
Vulgate. In Latin there is no article, and the distinction
apparent in Greek disappears. The word *homo* can mean
either 'mankind' or 'an individual man', but its apposi-
tion to *deus* (God) in this verse suggests the former meaning. True, the word *homo* is used in the previous verse
to mean 'husband', and it is also used five verses later
by the disciples in the same sense, and an attention to
context and the nature of the question put to Christ,
would point to the same meaning of *homo* in this verse.
But the other interpretation is, in Latin, grammatically
possible, and it became universally accepted in the West.
This gave a Biblical justification for the rejection of the
Matthean exception.

Moreover, such an interpretation at the time of the formation of Canon Law in the eleventh and following centuries was admirably suited to the establishment of Papal power in face of the growing rivalry of the Emperor and the development of Civil Law. The only possible release from a marriage was by a decree of nullity, in which there was a final appeal to the Pope, while in some cases he had sole jurisdiction. This control gave the Pope an immense influence in Western Christendom, and a complete supremacy over national Churches, to whom was allowed no power of dispensation.

From this Western interpretation of Christian marriage human nature demanded a loophole of escape, and this was found in decrees of nullity, based chiefly on marriage within the forbidden degrees of affinity. Under the pressure of human frailty the forbidden degrees of affinity became so extended, and their application so unpredictable, as to create a threat to the stability of marriage itself that was never created by controlled divorce. Moreover, the intricacy of the marriage law gave an immense advantage to wealth unscrupulously used.

We have attempted in this chapter to show that the evidence of the New Testament and the practice of the Early Church bear another interpretation than that which has been put upon them in support of the Resolutions of Convocation. The realization that the Greek original of the familiar words of Christ, on which is based the Western conception of the indissolubility of marriage, could not bear that meaning and were not so understood by the Early Church, throws a clear light on the great difference in this matter between the East and the West. The problem in the East was to relate to the frailty of human nature Christ's denial of the right of husband or wife to dissolve their marriage by putting away their partner at their own will, at a time when this was the normal form of divorce. The answer to the problem was given by Christ Himself in the Matthean exception, 'except for fornication', by which He permitted a divorce in this form in circumstances which were approved by a God-fearing law. This principle was followed, 'in Christ's spirit', by St Paul; then, more uncertainly, in the early centuries by episcopal dispensations; and finally, in the sixth century, by the Code of Justinian, permitting divorce and remarriage on grounds laid down by a Christian state authority. From the first the grounds were not limited to adultery.

This was the interpretation of Christ's teaching on marriage and divorce during the first millennium of Christianity. How this conception came to be altered in the West by a new interpretation of Christ's words, we have now seen. In the East divorce was accepted on certain grounds, and the problem was remarriage. In the West marriage was declared to be indissoluble, and therefore divorce was impossible and the problem of remarriage did not arise.

IV

The Church of England

The abuse of the process of nullity was one of the foremost scandals of the Church in the eyes of the Protestant Reformers. On the Continent it provoked a reaction which established absolute divorce in place of legal separation (divorce *a mensa et thoro*). In England the prohibited degrees of affinity were drastically reduced, thus reducing the grounds for a decree of nullity and the possibility of escape from a wrecked marriage. A Commission was appointed under Henry VIII and Edward VI, for the Reformation of Ecclesiastical Laws, in order to draw up a Code to provide for the granting of absolute divorce, as on the Continent, but the death of Edward and the accession of Mary prevented its passing into law. Nevertheless, there developed a widespread assumption of the right to remarriage after divorce for adultery, and a Canon of 1603 had to reassert that such a divorce was only a legal separation, and that the Ecclesiastical Courts had no power to grant an absolute divorce.

Under the Commonwealth, the practice of Continental Protestantism was followed, and, though the canonical authority was restored after the Restoration, the right of absolute divorce for adultery was made possible by a specific Act of Parliament in each case. This was only available to the richest classes, and the impossibility of divorce for the nation as a whole was a major cause of the moral laxity of the eighteenth century. Amongst the upper classes marital infidelity was tolerated and often openly admitted, and, for those who resented it, the duel took the place of the divorce court. In the lower classes sexual immorality was rampant and illicit unions were accepted as matters of course.

At last, in the middle of the nineteenth century, the situation was felt to be intolerable, and in 1857 the Matrimonial Causes Act transferred jurisdiction in matrimonial matters from the Ecclesiastical Courts to the State, and granted an absolute divorce to a husband on the ground of his wife's adultery, and to the wife on the grounds of adultery and cruelty on the part of her husband.

There was opposition on the part of the High Church party, but there was considerable support from the Church generally, including Bishop Tait of London and other bishops, and a general acceptance of the remarriage in church of divorced persons. A concession was made to the opposition by permitting any clergyman to refuse to perform himself the remarriage of a guilty party.

The general acceptance by the Church in the nineteenth century is manifest in the two declarations of the Lambeth Conference, which I have already quoted, covering a space of twenty years (1888 and 1908), discountenancing any exclusion from Holy Communion of those remarried after divorce. It is true that the opinion of the Lambeth Conference moved steadily in the next thirty years in the direction of a more rigorist attitude towards the remarriage in church of the innocent party. It must be borne in mind, however, that the Anglican

Communion is not identical with the Church of England by law established in this land. A certain discipline may have to be followed in a place where the Church is an extreme minority in a non-Christian community, with a non-Christian government, or with a British administration that rightly takes cognizance of the overwhelming non-Christian majority. Such a discipline is by no means applicable to the situation confronting the Church of England, which is the national Church of a country that, by a great majority, would call itself Christian, with a government which completely accepts the Christian ideal of lifelong marriage. It grants divorce, not to depreciate this ideal, but to meet the consequences of the human failure or refusal to live up to it, and to relieve a situation which, humanly speaking, is bound to result in an increase in immorality and a consequent abandonment of religion.

The Lambeth Conference expresses the opinions of the bishops of the whole Anglican Communion, and on matters of faith and morals carries great weight; but matters of discipline are the concern of the local churches. Moreover, in the Church of England discipline is not settled by the bishops alone, but by bishops and clergy sitting in Convocation and acting canonically with the consent of the Sovereign and the agreement of the law. It is difficult to see how the opinion of the bishops in the Lambeth Conference on a matter of discipline can be called 'official church opinion'.

Another cause contributed to the stiffening of opinion in Convocation itself, in the thirties, against the re-marriage of the innocent party in church. For eighty years after 1857 adultery remained the only ground for divorce in England, though there was a widespread feeling from the beginning of the century that other causes, which made a true marriage impossible, should be taken into account, and in 1912 a very strong Commission stressed the urgency of this. In 1923 simple adultery was made a ground of divorce for wife as well as husband. This was an act of common justice, which the feminist movement, greatly strengthened by the First World War, made it impossible to resist. But inasmuch as no provision was made for other grounds for divorce, this measure brought great discredit to all divorce procedure, for it provoked the practice of divorce by collusion. It is strange that English law, having admitted divorce, should have continued for so long a time with adultery as the sole ground, when, in the New Testament, the Early Church, and in the divorce *a mensa et thoro* of the Roman Church, other grounds had always been admitted.

In 1937 Sir Alan Herbert's 'Matrimonial Causes Act' added the grounds of wilful desertion, cruelty and incurable insanity. It also took steps to prevent collusion. Later, legal aid was granted to those unable to meet the expense of divorce proceedings.

Those who take the rigorist view often speak of the Matrimonial Causes Measure of 1937 as the action of the State taken in defiance of the Church. It is as well to remember that while some bishops in the House of Lords uncompromisingly attacked the Measure, others, including Bishop Hensley Henson, spoke strongly in support of it, both from a Christian and a social point of view. Meanwhile the two Archbishops, Lang and Temple, declared that, while they felt that in their office they could not vote in favour of the Measure, they would not vote against it, on the ground that they thought that it ought to be passed (in the words of Archbishop Temple), 'for the reason that it will improve rather than damage public morals'.

It must appear to a large number of people a bewildering attitude for a National Church to take up, which by its constitution is related to the life of the whole nation. To inform Parliament that the measure of relief it is proposing *ought* to be granted *on moral grounds*, and at the same time to declare that any members of the National Church that availed themselves of this relief would be deprived of the right to be married sacramentally in their parish church, and would be controlled in their admission to Holy Communion, must appear to most thinking people morally confusing. It imposes a grievous penalty on church people who, like the Archbishops, felt that this was a necessary, desirable Measure.

A great deal is said about divorce from the point of view of the upper and middle classes. In the debate in the House of Lords, two of the law lords, with long experience of the divorce courts, pointed out that the problem weighed most heavily upon the working classes. If a working man is deserted by an unfaithful wife and perhaps left with children, he is bound to find some woman to look after them and to minister to his own domestic needs. Unless he can divorce his wife *and marry again*, he will almost inevitably live in illicit relations with some other woman. Indeed, it was the indignant sarcasm of a judge, a century ago, called upon to try on the charge of bigamy a man in just such a situation, that created the national demand for the 1857 Measure. The Church of England is already too much alienated from the life of the majority of working men, without setting up a rigid attitude to divorce and remarriage that can only widen the gulf. One cannot but remember some other words of Christ, 'Ye bind heavy burdens and grievous to be borne and lay them on men's shoulders.'

Now, one of the grounds given for the return of Convocation to the rigid approach to marriage and divorce is the steady increase in the number of divorces since 1857. But this does not prove the moral degeneracy of the nation. Obviously, the granting of the right of divorce and, subsequently, of increased grounds *must* mean an increase in divorces. If one feels it necessary to open the sluices of a dam, one expects more water to flow through. That is the object in opening them. The granting of facilities for divorce is based on the conviction that there are many people suffering under an intolerable relationship in their marriage, of which they ought to be able to be free, if they wish. This *must be expected* to result in an increase in the number of divorces. So too, the putting of women on an equality with men and the enabling of the poor to have the same opportunities as the rich must result in a further increase. But these grounds are given from a sense of justice and compassion and, except on the basis of the Western interpretation of Christ's words, no one could dissent from them. Those who deplore divorce speak as though the alternative would be ordered Christian homes. The alternative would be the same conditions that we saw existed in the eighteenth century.

The contention that permission for divorce lowers the morality of a country is disproved by the fact that in Scotland the right of divorce for adultery or desertion has existed for 300 years. Yet the sexual morality of Scotland has not been lower than that of England, and in the eighteenth century it was higher.

In the past century we have witnessed several of what

Justinian described as the great changes through which humanity passes. The year 1870, from which time statistics are often taken, marks the beginning of two great changes in the life of our nation. In the first place universal education was established. This brought to the masses, who to a great extent lived at a very low level, with no hope of improvement, a new sense of personality, a self-consciousness which more and more claimed the right to self-fulfilment in a good life.

The other movement was equally potent, the emancipation of woman. The rigid attitude to divorce bears far more heavily on woman than on man. In the nineteenth century, a man separated from his wife because of her infidelity enjoyed a freedom and an absence of criticism because of his circumstances. To a woman, that was never granted. Separation meant a cramped, frustrated social life. It is for this reason that in Roman Catholic countries so many women tolerate infidelity for the sake of their social position, and marriage and love tend to be regarded as separate states.

Moreover, before 1870 the majority of women were far less educated than their husbands, and therefore without any means of economic independence. All that has changed, and the unwillingness of women to accept the conditions of subjection to an unfaithful or cruel husband is one of the chief causes of the increase in divorce.

Both these movements carry dangers and are in need of guidance and self-control, but their effect on the problem of marriage and divorce is due as much to moral indignation as to self-indulgence. When one adds to these causes the fact of two devastating wars, which shattered, as they always will shatter, the stability of marriage, one is not so much surprised at the increase in divorces, as at the fact that, even now, *only six to seven out of every hundred marriages are terminated by divorce*.[1] One cannot describe this as a condition of national moral collapse. No one can minimize the tragic results of divorce, especially to children; but there are just as great, if not so obvious, tragedies involved for both parents and children in the rigid attitude to this question.

Finally, there has been another result of these two movements, and that is the growth throughout this century, in Western humanity, of a romantic attitude towards marriage. We are so familiar with it that we do not realize how different it is from the attitude that has prevailed in past centuries, and that still persists today amongst other peoples.

As a result of the rigid attitude of the Western Church towards divorce, there grew up through the centuries a separation in men's minds between the love relationship between man and woman and the regularized institution of marriage, based on family and economic considerations. This came to its most blatant expression in the eighteenth century, in the Age of Reason. Marriage must needs be endured, however it turn out, but love was satisfied in extra-marital relationships.

In this century, with the release of the individual from economic and family control, and with the relaxation of the rigidity of the marriage bond, marriage has been re-invested in men's minds with its proper quality of love. It is felt that the romance of love between a man and a woman should find its natural expression in marriage. The very demand for the possibility of divorce is itself an indication of this. There is always, in every age, a

[1] Royal Commission on Marriage and Divorce, p. 369.

section of wealthy, pleasure-loving people who seek satisfaction in promiscuous, self-indulgent sex-adventure. But the majority of people today have not that amoral attitude to marriage that characterized the eighteenth century. They are not satisfied with promiscuous sex-relationships; they seek happiness in marriage, in the belief that in marriage an enduring personal relationship of love is to be found. If their marriage breaks down, they demand the possibility of divorce, and the right to look for such a relationship in another marriage. It is an attitude fraught with the dangers of selfishness and superficial sentimentality, and only too often results in disappointment and disillusionment. But beneath it is the belief that human loneliness can only be resolved in a love-relationship, which finds its true expression in marriage. According to Nicholas Berdyaev, it is the great problem which mankind today is trying to solve.

Such an attitude enormously increases the problem of sex-relationship in marriage. In this the Church gives little assistance. She declares that the first object of marriage is child-bearing, the second is as an outlet for physical desire, the third is for the mutual companionship and comfort which each finds in the other. But this is not the romantic search for a unique, satisfying love-relationship with an individual of the opposite sex, which is dominant in the minds of those entering upon marriage. It may be said truly that the words of betrothal express this unique personal love, and there is little doubt that those who use them feel this in speaking them. All the more is it a tragedy that, when the fault of one of them makes the continuance of that relationship impossible, words, which were uttered as a free and sincere act of love, have become a legalistic formula within which each party is imprisoned, for as long as the entirely separated existence of the other lasts.

Any concern with sex-relationship that goes behind or beyond the three declared objects of marriage is suspect, and in some Churches utterly condemned. But, as Berdyaev puts it, 'People marry, not because they want to beget children, but because of irresistible desire, because they love and are in love, because they want to be united to the loved one.' If mankind in general mistakes selfishness, infatuation and sex-satisfaction for true personal love, yet in its heart that is what it is seeking, and the Church gives little guidance and understanding in this, if she regards with suspicion, if not dislike, the physical union in which the love of man and woman finds its natural expression.

When Christ set out the divine principle behind marriage, on which the Church claims to base her own attitude, He based it entirely on the sex-relationship, seen in the light of a divine purpose. He said nothing about child-bearing, nor expressed any condemnation of the sex-instinct. He taught clearly that it was God's purpose that mankind should arrive at the fullness of being, at the overcoming of the loneliness of physical existence, in the love of man and woman.

Sex-relationship is the divinely ordained physical means to this end. It is a mystery which the belief in the material origin of man and the animal evolution of sex can never comprehend or achieve, but because man is spirit, he will never let it go. The fundamental element in the sex-relationship, as ordained by God, is the fusion of man and woman as spirit beings in a physical union. Only a Church untainted by a materialistic concept of man's being can help mankind to understand this mystery. We shall attempt in the final chapter to consider it more deeply.

We stand today at one of the turning-points in the history of mankind, that expresses itself in great changes in humanity. Nothing can stem these changes, and it is the task of the Church to recognize them and be ready to help and guide them.

One would have thought that this moment offered a great opportunity for the Church of England to follow the example of the Orthodox Church and to co-operate with the State, which, accepting Christ's standard of life-long marriage and the impossibility of its being dissolved by the arbitrary will of the husband or wife, is seeking to meet, in that spirit, the conditions created in human romanticism by human sin and failure; to give release and provide the possibility of a fresh start, and at the same time to do all that is possible to strengthen in the nation the stability of marriage. That purpose the report of the recent Royal Commission on Marriage and Divorce expresses in these words: 'We do not think that the remedy for the problem of marriage failure lies in making divorce more difficult. The roots of the evil go too deep for such a course to be effective. We are convinced that the real remedy lies in other directions.'

Those who dissent from the present attitude of Convocation feel that it sets the Church in opposition to the State, in an attitude of disapproval. By her radical opposition to the main plan of State reform, namely, legally controlled divorce, the Church is establishing a gulf between herself and the State which will inevitably widen. The nation as a whole will feel itself out of touch with a Church, whose approach to one of its deepest and most urgent problems is a reactionary rigidity, which has been abandoned by other Christian Churches here and abroad.

Moreover, a barrier will be raised to the reunion of the Church of England with these other Churches, towards which she has been working more hopefully in recent years. They are equally conscious with ourselves of the problems of marriage and divorce and the social dangers arising from them, but they will find it very difficult to be united to a Church which is abandoning its century-old approach to the attitude which they believe to be right, and has turned its face again towards the medieval pattern.

It is difficult to see why, in this matter, we should return to the attitude of the Roman Church. In the opinion of Bishop Creighton, 'the Church of Rome showed itself at its worst in its treatment of the problem of marriage and divorce'. Possibly, no other ecclesiastical pronouncement has brought more unhappiness and frustration to Christendom than the Papal pronouncement of the indissolubility of marriage as the declaration of Christ. While it maintained rigidly the principle of marriage as an indissoluble, lifelong union, the Church of Rome was averse to the sex instinct, and it did little to produce the true ideals of sex-relationship in marriage. Its rigidity provoked a widespread disregard of marital fidelity, and resulted in perverse reactions against sex-repression, that affected even the highest Orders in the Church. It is often claimed that it established the Christian ideal of the family and the home, but there is little evidence for this. In practice, the standard of family life and the treatment of children in medieval Western Christendom did not equal that of the Eastern Church under Byzantine rule, nor that of the Jews in Europe itself. The hypocrisy and chicanery with which the process of nullity was made an easy substitute for divorce for those who could pay for it, corrupted the morals of rich and poor alike. Moreover, in almost all countries where the rigid attitude to divorce prevails, there is inevitably highly organized prostitution. The social and political history of Europe would have been vastly happier had Justinian's sane and enlightened legislation on marriage and divorce prevailed in the Western Church, as it did in the Eastern.

If the interpretation of Christ's words in the New Testament and of the practice of the Early Church, given in the previous chapter, is accepted, there is no longer any need to establish the principle of the indissolubility of marriage at the cost of great human suffering and frustration, for no such principle was laid down by Christ; nor of the principle of the lifelong nature of marriage, for that is accepted by both Church and State. The Christ-taught principle of the impossibility of divorce at the will of husband or wife, and its control by a recognized Christian authority, is enshrined and established in the law of this land. Although, in popular parlance, we speak of one partner divorcing the other, this is not really correct. All that can be done, under British law, is for one partner to petition the Court, on the ground of submitted evidence, to grant to him or her the dissolution of the marriage. This is quite different from one partner 'putting away' the other at their own will, which Christ declared to be no dissolution, and therefore as involving adultery in the event of remarriage. The legal process in England is on a par with the legislation of Justinian. It has, of course, different grounds for divorce, as would be expected in a quite different age, but these grounds were accepted by Parliament—and also by Archbishops Lang and Temple—as morally justifiable. Even divorce on the ground of three years' separation is not divorce by mutual consent, as some assert it to be. It is evidence to the Court of such inveterate incompatibility as to make the marriage no longer possible, and on that ground the Court dissolves the marriage.

There is therefore no justification for the pastoral discipline of church people, merely on the ground of remarriage after divorce in this country. There may well be circumstances, which are the background or accompaniment of such a divorce or remarriage, which demand disciplinary treatment, but that can be initiated in the normal Prayer Book way in each case.

We have also tried to show that the symptoms of our time, disquieting though they are, are not indications of a general moral collapse, but are the birth-pangs of a new era. This calls to the Church, not for the assertion of absolute principles by an external rigidity of discipline, but for the full sharing of the fierce problems, where they confront humanity. Some thoughts on how this might be achieved will occupy the next chapter.

V

An Alternative Approach

※

The fundamental disagreement that many Church people feel with the approach to this problem that finds expression in these Resolutions of Convocation, does not imply that they think that the Church should sit back and let matters take their course, marrying all divorced persons in church without any question, and contenting herself with general expressions of disapproval of the way things are drifting. The increase in the number of broken marriages is a tragedy, not only for the persons concerned, for their children, and for Society as a whole, but especially for the Church, which has stood for the principle of lifelong marriage which Christ taught, for nearly 2,000 years, in various ways and with varying success. It is a problem with which she must grapple closely and directly.

The real weakness of the present Resolutions of Convocation is that in them the Church is not brought into contact with this problem in people's lives at the vital point where the marriage is beginning to break up. The preparation for marriage is now far more generally used than in the past, but it does not meet the problem. In the first place, its efficacy depends entirely upon the clergyman who gives it, and some feel themselves quite unfitted for this task. Nor is there any certainty that the

F

preparation is given at all. In any case the man and woman concerned are usually in a state where the possibility of a breakdown in their marriage seems to them incredible, if not impossible, and if the preparation does not offend them, it often makes little impression. Undoubtedly, a wise and understanding clergyman can give in his preparation spiritual and moral teaching and inspiration that may colour all their life together. Still, it does not admit the Church to the real place where the battle is fought.

So too, the suggested pastoral discipline of those who are remarried after divorce, even if it were of use, comes too late. The marriage has already broken down in divorce, and, if they are the sort of people who 'desire' to receive Holy Communion, it is more than likely that they found their spiritual recovery long before remarriage and have been communicants since their divorce. Even where there has not been that deep experience, time has healed the wounds of the former tragedy and has brought to them a new love and the possibility of a happy second marriage. That the Church, which has very often made no actual contact with their marriage problems since the priest's exhortations at a former marriage, should now apply this pastoral discipline, seems to them, if not offensive, wrongly timed and out of place, and above all too late.

What is needed is that church people should be made to recognize that, if they are married in church and with Christian rites, *they have involved the Church in the sanctity of their vows, and, if their marriage breaks down, the Church is involved in their tragedy*. It is therefore their duty to seek the help of the Church at the first threat of such a breakdown. When their own love and patience seem unable to retrieve the situation and they are drifting apart, one or both should bring the matter before their parish priest or the bishop, seeking—if they so wish, under the seal of secrecy—his counsel and help. There are, of course, Marriage Guidance Councils, but they are generally contacted at a later stage, and there is an element of wider publicity in them than in a confidential approach to their recognized spiritual counsellor, representing the Church whose standards are involved in the stability of their marriage. In some cases, however, it might well be that the priest or bishop would put his consultant in touch with a Marriage Guidance Council.

Very important results would follow from such an early approach to the Church. In the first place, there would be the opportunity of helping the offended party to look at the situation from a really Christian angle. Very often the wronged party is led to say or do things, at the first wounding of love or pride, which inevitably widen the breach, and may make reconciliation far more difficult. At this stage a wise spiritual counsellor can suggest an attitude of mind and a line of action, that would be far more effective than anything possible at a later stage. Secondly, the bishop would know from the start who is the innocent party and who it is who wishes to keep the marriage intact. Moreover, if the matter eventually reached the Court, the evidence of such early approach to the Church would carry great weight as to the real innocence of the petitioner.

Thirdly, the spiritual counsel would be a continuous process, when and where it was really needed, and would remove any necessity for a report and moral assessment of the situation when it was all over, as is now proposed.

Fourthly, it would result in a great reduction in the

number of divorces. It must have been the experience of many priests, as it has been mine, to have been able to save marriages from ending in divorce, because one has been able to intervene at an early stage. Nothing is more rewarding than the thankfulness in later years of those whose marriages have been saved.

Finally, it would provide the Church with an adequate means of expressing its faith in Christ's principle of life-long marriage, in a way that would win the moral approval even of those who do not hold her standards, and would not inflict on anyone the sense of uncharitable and undeserved censure.

Clearly, if church people are married with the rites and blessing of the Church, whose standards are clearly set out in the marriage service itself, and then suffer their marriage to break up *without giving the Church any opportunity to save it*, they cannot expect the Church to believe that they really hold these standards, nor to allow them to be remarried with the same Church rites and blessing. I do not suggest that this discipline should be applied with rigidity, as compulsion or timidity might have prevented such an approach to the Church, and there should be room for real penitence for having neglected to do this. But it could be recognized that normally the Church would not admit to another marriage in Church those who had suffered the break-up of their former marriage, without seeking the Church's help and counsel. Nothing would have more effect in inducing Christian people always to make this approach, with the most far-reaching results in restoring the stability of marriage in the nation.

Such a recognition, however, could only be brought about if the Church admitted the possibility of remarriage after divorce, and for the innocent party and, in special circumstances, for others, the possibility of re-marriage in Church. I am not suggesting uniformity of practice in this respect; there should be complete free-dom of conscience for those who cannot feel that this is right. But it does involve an alteration in the attitude of the Resolutions of Convocation. Most people would not consider approaching the Church if they knew they would be met, in many instances by the assertion that nothing ever justifies an absolute divorce, and in all cases by the attitude that remarriage in Church is out of the question, and that any remarriage would be considered wrong in principle, and be subject to pastoral inquiry and discipline.

Furthermore, it is necessary, if this responsibility for seeking the help and Counsel of the Church is to be recognized by those who are married, that the promise should be made, or the charge given, at the marriage service itself. As long ago as 1938 a proposal was put forward in the Lower House of Convocation of the insertion of a new promise in the Marriage Service to this effect.

> 'Do you promise that, if anything should seem to threaten the possibility of keeping the solemn promises which you have made to one another, then as soon as possible, and in any case before resort is made to the law, you will take counsel of your parish priest or the bishop?

Considerable sympathy was expressed with the proposal, but it was turned down because it would mean an alteration in the marriage service, which might involve proceedings which would postpone for a long time the proposed measures of pastoral discipline.

The matter was raised again in Convocation in 1956, and as a result this final clause was added to the resolutions on pastoral discipline.

'Recognizing that pastoral care may well avert the danger of divorce, if it comes into play before legal proceedings have been started, this House urges all clergy, in their preparation of couples for marriage, to tell them, both for their own sakes and for that of their friends, that the good offices of the clergy are always available.'

To my mind this is quite inadequate for establishing this consultation as a regular procedure, and as the generally recognized test of the sincerity in the persons concerned of their acceptance of Christ's standard in marriage. It is only advice to the clergy, it suffers from the limitations in the effectiveness of preparation to which I have referred, and it lacks the solemnity and weight of a personal promise or a direct charge delivered at the marriage ceremony.

The wording of any such promise or charge would be a matter for careful drafting by Convocation, and the following draft of a charge is merely given to express what I have in mind. It could be given to the whole congregation present, so as to avoid any appearance of a personal warning to the bride and bridegroom. It might form the conclusion of the general introduction to the service, and would add to the solemnity of the taking of the marriage vows immediately afterwards.

'Dearly beloved, the solemn vows and promises, which those who are married in church make each to the other in the sight of God, are not only of deep concern to themselves, but also to the whole Church, through whom they have been brought into this holy estate of matrimony. It is therefore incumbent upon those who are married, if at any time circumstances should arise which appear to them to threaten the stability of their marriage, that as soon as possible, and before any other action is taken, they should seek counsel and advice on the matter from their parish priest or the bishop or someone appointed by him. Those who suffer their marriage to break down without giving the Church the opportunity of helping them to preserve it, cannot be regarded by the Church as holding in their hearts with any sincerity their responsibility as Christians towards Christ's ideal of marriage, which the Church accepts and to which they themselves expressed adherence in this service; nor as church people towards the Church to which they belong and with whose rites they were married.'

There are some who are averse to such a reference to the possibility of divorce at the marriage service, as being out of keeping with its spirit. Such an attitude overlooks the fact that there are two explicit references to divorce in the present form of service. In these days it is quite unreal that a marriage should be solemnized in complete disregard of such a possibility. It is far better to issue the warning and point to the remedy at the marriage service itself, when the vows are about to be taken, than to try to impose a discipline, when an irrevocable breakdown has occurred.

For those who accept the meaning of Christ's words which is given in this book there would be involved certain slight changes in the marriage service; but changes are already allowed, for example, in omitting the word 'obey' in the betrothal, and also in the actual words of marriage. Only two further changes would be involved. Cranmer's translation of Our Lord's words at the joining of hands would have to be permissibly altered to some such form as this.

'You whom God hath joined together let neither of you put asunder.'

Or

'The union into which God hath brought you, let neither of you break.'

The other words come in one of the collects:

'that it should never be lawful to put asunder those whom Thou by matrimony hast made one.'

These words might read:

'It should never be lawful for either of those whom Thou by matrimony hast made one, to dissolve this unity.'

This, however, which it was so necessary to say and teach in Our Lord's day, is now recognized by the law of most Christian lands, and the phrase might be omitted in using the collect.

These permissions, additions, and changes in the marriage service would be the logical consequence of the fresh approach to the problem which I have suggested. The purpose of this approach is that the Church should not content herself with preliminary warning and consequential discipline, but should force her way to the heart of the conflict. By her pastoral care for her sons and daughters in the hour of their spiritual need and by a compassionate attitude to human frailty, she will bear a more effective witness to her concern for Christ's standard of marriage, than by a rigid assertion of a principle and a belated application of a dubious form of discipline. Moreover, by avoiding a gulf of principle between herself and the State, in its constant attempt to reconcile Christian standards with the actual immediate possibilities of ordinary men and women, she will gain a new influence in State legislation, that will prevent it from falling into the hands of those who have no regard for the Christian view of marriage.

VI

Freedom and Authority

For the past three centuries the special characteristic of the Church of England has been that she has stood for the spiritual freedom of the individual, and for the belief in liberty of thought and interpretation. The issue between spiritual freedom and spiritual authority has been present from the beginning in the Christian Church. It was the issue between St Paul, who stood for freedom, and the Jewish Christians, who stood for complete obedience to the law.

There are some stages in human development when absolute spiritual authority is a necessity for mankind. St Paul spoke of the Jewish law as a necessary schoolmaster for the souls of men in the pre-Christian world. So too was it necessary that in the Dark Ages the Church of Rome should be the schoolmaster of Europe. When in the Age of Reason in the fifteenth and sixteenth centuries adolescence awoke in the European peoples, the schoolmaster could only believe in applying yet more rigidly the discipline of childhood, and the Reformation was the result. The chief characteristic of the Reformation in this country was the claim for the spiritual freedom of the individual, but for two centuries the incapacity of those who desired freedom for themselves, to respect the same desire in others caused perpetual religious strife. In the eighteenth century toleration, and in the nineteenth century comprehensiveness, became the accepted principle of the Church of England, and it was in this spirit that the Marriage Act of 1857 was passed and administered. There was respect for the many varying viewpoints; for the rigorist point of view in the exemption of any clergyman who objected to the necessity of marrying a divorced person, and for different interpretations of scripture, and for individual decisions of conscience. This attitude was expressed in this resolution of the Lambeth Conference in 1888.

'Recognizing the fact that there has always been difference of opinion in the Church on the question whether Our Lord meant to forbid marriage to the innocent party in a divorce for adultery, the Conference recommends that the Clergy should not be instructed to refuse the sacraments or other privileges of the Church to those who, under civil sanction, are thus married.'

This characteristic principle in the Church of England is well set out by Canon Roger Lloyd in his book, *The Church of England in the Twentieth Century*.

'Where our system, as exemplified in the Book of Common Prayer and enshrined in centuries of history, differs most strongly from that of the Roman Catholic and the Orthodox Churches, is in the tremendous emphasis it places on the spiritual freedom of the individual. Throughout the whole range of our worship and our life, the permissive "You may" or "You should" predominates over the dominical "You must". The Prayer Book says "You must" to the clergy in the ordering of public worship, and in the recitation of the Daily Offices of Morning and Evening Prayer. It says "You must" to the laity *only* in the matter of communicating three times in the year, including Easter Day.'

Perhaps this spirit of freedom and comprehensiveness is most clearly expressed in the Preface to the 1928 Prayer Book, which was the fruit of years of intense effort in all three parties in the Church to understand one another's point of view. Speaking of the evolution of freedom in our English life, the Preface said:

'Not less strange to the men of the age of Elizabeth or Charles II would have seemed a model of government in Church and State which guards instead of mistrusting liberty of thought and speech, and would set no narrower bounds to freedom than those which belong to brotherhood and fellowship. In religion, as in all else, truth is not prized less highly because it is no longer fenced on any side.'

It was, in a way, the close of a period. The unexpected rejection of the Prayer Book by Parliament set up in some quarters a sense of opposition between Church and State, and a determination to assert the Church's point of view. When in 1938 there came out the long-delayed Report of the Commission on the Doctrine of the Church of England appointed in 1922, its comprehensiveness and freedom from party dogmatism provoked a good deal of criticism and opposition, not only from outside the Church but from within it.

It was clear that a movement was growing for closing the ranks of the Church of England on matters of faith and practice, by the exercise of a stricter spiritual discipline. There had already started the debates in Convocation on the Report on Marriage and Divorce. The Report was clearly coloured by the alarm at the increase in the number of divorces, and demanded a change of policy and more drastic action. The traditional belief in spiritual freedom, however, was still vigorous and there was a strong feeling in both Houses of the Canterbury Convocation against rigid action. The proposal to refuse Communion to any who had married after divorce was rejected by the Lower House by a large majority, and the House refused to consider at that stage any measure of discipline against remarriage. Perhaps one of the most striking statements on the Report was made by Archbishop Lang himself. 'In my judgment', he said, 'it would be a much too confident assertion to lay down, as has been laid down in the Commission's Report, that where there has been full consent on both sides and the marriage has been consummated, the marriage is for life, and, as a consequence, it is against the will of God for Christian men and women to remarry during the lifetime of the former spouse.'

When Convocation resumed after the war, it proceeded almost at once to the formation of a new set of canons, and it was clear that a more authoritarian point of view was asserting itself. A startling illustration of this was the presentation in the Church Assembly in 1947 of the Report of a Committee on 'The Spiritual Discipline of the Laity'. The Report stated that 'the duties which are *imposed upon* all lay members of the Church of England without any exception and are *universally obligatory*', include attendance at divine service on every Sunday and Holy Day throughout the year, and the observance of all the appointed fasting days, including every Friday. It set out a formidable list of obligatory duties, which were to be enforced by spiritual discipline.

In spite of some speeches of protest, the Report was received with general acclamation by the Assembly, and was committed to Convocation for implementation. It was pressed relentlessly in Convocation by the rigorists, but they met with strong opposition and had finally to yield to the practical wisdom of the Upper House, which did not relish the task of attempting spiritual coercion on such a scale! A far less exacting list of Christian duties was drawn up by the Archbishops, in a spirit of exhortation, rather than of command.

Needless to say, the belief in freedom and comprehensiveness is still strong in the Church, and has been raised successfully on many occasions in the post-war debates. On the other hand, the recent Act of Convocation in regard to Marriage and Divorce is a clear step in the authoritarian direction. The reversal of the attitude of the Church towards State legislation on marriage and divorce from that which had been followed for a century by all but a small section, and the attempt to force this new attitude upon the Church by the majority vote of bishops and clergy in Convocation, without any real consultation with church people as a whole, and in the face of an admittedly large dissenting minority, is a clear instance of the growing tendency to substitute for the freedom of minorities their subjection to rule by majority vote. One cannot but contrast the unwillingness of the Lower House of Canterbury Convocation in 1938, even to consider any discipline against remarriage after divorce, in view of the division of opinion both in Convocation and in the country on the subject, with the present authoritarian resentment at any dissent from the present Resolutions.

It is impossible to imagine that Convocation will consider any reconsideration of its Resolutions at the present time, but if it finds a considerable minority in opposition to them, the Church should suffer these two approaches to the problem of divorce and remarriage to exist side by side without rancour, as they did for 100 years. It may be that the knowledge that the words of Christ, which seem to pronounce the indissolubility of marriage, were not used in that sense, and were not so understood in the Early Church, may release many from a scruple of conscience that has reluctantly compelled them to take the rigid view.

If, however, the Church authorities refuse any compromise, the only line of opposition for those who are in conscience opposed to them is to rely upon the fact that this Act of Convocation is not canonically binding, and to refuse to be bound by its Resolutions, in the hope that all those who agree with this point of view will do likewise, and take all steps they can to resist any attempt to enforce them. It is a strange thing that it should be thought to be wrong that some clergy, in obedience to their conscience, should still claim the right to marry a person in Church after divorce, in dissent from the opinion of the majority—when the same possibility of dissent has been enjoyed by others for 100 years, to refrain from taking such marriages, when the Church as a whole did so.

It is a very unpleasant situation to feel compelled actively to oppose the expressed opinion of a large and official majority, but it is the only alternative to acquiescing in the Church taking up a reactionary attitude to this great problem, which will more and more put it out of touch with the nation. It remains to be seen whether the as yet unconsulted mass of clergy and church people has the desire and the will to express sufficient dissent to make Convocation look again at the problem.

This issue of spiritual freedom is of supreme importance to church people, quite apart from its relation to the question of marriage and divorce. The attraction to an authoritarian Church is very strong, particularly in times of unrest and uncertainty, and when spiritual principles are threatened on many sides. Such a Church can issue its commands and make its decisions quickly and effectively, without any of the delays imposed by a more democratic procedure. It gives comfort and security, for it relieves its followers of the responsibility of making difficult decisions. It is easier to be told what books you may read, what television programmes you may look at, what you are to believe and what you are to do—and to assure yourself that whatever you are told must be right.

But all this takes no cognizance of the development of humanity. Mankind cannot return to the age of childhood, nor even of adolescence. It is advancing into manhood, in the case of some peoples, almost at one leap from childhood. More and more conscious of its selfhood, and by turns arrogant and bewildered, it has to face the necessity of making decisions on the perplexing issues which confront it, in full freedom and responsibility. For this it needs a Church which believes in the spiritual freedom of the individual and its own responsibility for training him to use it; and holds to that belief, in spite of conflicting viewpoints, and only partly-achieved ideals, and the risk of sinners unworthily partaking of spiritual privileges; because she believes it is the way of Christ Himself with men and women.

VII

Marriage was Made for Man

It was pointed out in the Introduction that the title of this book does not belittle the sanctity of marriage. On the contrary, it implies that there are deep purposes of God for man, which find their realization in the life-long union of one man and one woman in marriage. In considering what those purposes are, we must beware of regarding them as evolving from the lower orders of nature by some process of enlightenment or intuition. Nothing has done more harm to the understanding of the nature of man and of the universe than the conception of evolution, by accident or the need of survival, from the lowest forms to the highest. We shall never understand the nature of man, nor the meaning of history, until we recognize in the process of evolution the conscious purpose of the spiritual world, and its continual attempt to express its forms and pattern of being more and more completely in a material medium. It is of course possible to trace the ascending perfection of this material expression, but the impetus for it is not derived from the side of matter, but from the incarnating activity of spirit, creatively shaping the material to be an ever more perfect expression of its aim.

For example, in regard to the sex-relationship, no one could conceive that the noble achievement of true love between man and wife must look for its source to some impulse hidden in the indiscriminate momentary mating of insects. Yet, even there spirit has been able to express the overwhelming power of mutual attraction, and, in higher orders of animal being, to incarnate abiding companionship, mother-love, and even, in some instances, wonderful examples of mutual fidelity. Even so, nothing does more harm than to attempt to explain to the young the significance of the sex-life of man and woman from the level of its manifestations in the animal world. Historians are beginning to realize in regard to man himself that his ideals and achievements are not the result of a blind struggle from an animal level, but that from the very beginning, man, as spirit, was guided and directed from out of the spiritual world, by those men who had been able to retain their connexion with it. The lower and more animal-like groups in the human race are not relics of man's earliest origin, but are the result of separation from this spiritual guidance and inspiration.

Especially is this the case in regard to marriage, for in almost every people, even those backward peoples amongst whom other laws are hardly defined, there are regulations about marriage, and they are closely interwoven with religion. This must always be borne in mind when one speaks of marriage from the point of view of 'the natural order'. This must never be taken to mean an instinctive natural law such as that which exists among animals, still less one that has evolved from a yet lower level, but it must always imply that universal regard for the sanctity of marriage as related to man's spiritual nature, which by higher guidance has always existed amongst mankind.

The Hebrews, with their intense belief in God as pure Spirit, held also the concept of the element of spirit in man, as derived from and returning to God. 'The spirit shall return unto God who gave it.'[1] We have already seen that with them marriage was ordered and controlled by the Sacred Law. There is a remarkable passage in the book of the prophet Malachi, written about the fifth century when, with the spread of monogamy, men were seeking to exercise their power of putting away their wife. For the most part the prophet is speaking in God's name to the people, but at some moments God is represented as speaking directly Himself, through the prophet's mouth.

'Ye covered with tears the altar of the Lord, and with weeping and groaning because of your troubles. But is it meet for me to have respect to your sacrifice or to receive anything as acceptable from your hands? Ye ask, "Wherefore?" Because the Lord hath borne witness between thee and the wife of thy youth, whom thou hast forsaken. Yet she was thy partner and the wife of thy covenant. Did she indeed behave unseemly? Yet there remained in her the residue of His spirit. But ye said, "What else doth God seek in marriage but seed?" Nay, take heed also to the spirit in which ye share, and forsake not the wife of thy youth. But if thou put away thy wife because thou dost hate her, saith the Lord God of Israel, then ungodliness is darkening thy counsel. Therefore give heed to the spirit that is between you, and forsake not thy wife.'[2]

When we turn to the teaching of Christ himself we can be certain that with him this spiritual concept of

[1] Eccles. xi. 7.   [2] Mal. ii. 13 (Septuagint version). See p. 50.

marriage was foremost. Whatever belief we may hold about his person, no one can deny that to him man was primarily a child of God with his origin and destiny in the spirit world. It is very significant that when he defines the true meaning of marriage he does not point to some ideal that lies in a future stage of evolution, but he speaks of a purpose and design of God in regard to marriage that has existed 'from the beginning'. When his hearers go back for their authority to Moses, he goes far behind Moses—'In the beginning it was not so.' 'In the beginning God made them male and female.' Thus he speaks of a purpose in marriage for man as spirit, and he declares that God had that purpose in His mind and prepared for it by this supreme act 'in the beginning'.

It is in the light of these words that we may try to understand what that great purpose for man is for which God prepared by the institution of marriage. 'In the beginning He *made them* male and female.' In other words God deliberately created this polarity of sex in human nature, with its tremendous urge upon each to come into union with the other. Man is spirit and the life of pure spirit is a state of continual intimate relationship and interpenetration of being. In that life of relationship spirit beings have their very existence. This is borne witness to by the mystics of every age, and of every creed or philosophy. But man, inasmuch as he is a being of earth, is a 'separated' being. He is cut off from the world in which he lives and from his fellow men by the very nature of his physical body and consciousness. It is in that 'separated' consciousness, in the feeling of 'I and thou', of himself as subject and the world as object, that man finds his own selfhood, that he discovers himself.

But though man *discovers* himself in his separatedness, he can never *fulfil* himself in it, for, as spirit-being, he requires for his full existence manifold inter-relationships.

'For this cause God made them male and female.' God *created* this polarity within humanity, in which a man and a woman, each aware of themselves as separate individuals, are drawn, by the sex-instinct in their physical organism and the love-instinct in their soul-nature, into the most intimate relationship both of body and soul. As earthly beings this mutual attraction, this love-relationship, seeks to express itself and finds its fulfilment in the intimacy of the physical sex-relationship, which God 'made in the beginning', in order that through it man might experience the life of spirit, the true spirit-nature of his being, in his 'separated' existence. This divinely-revealed function of the sex-relationship in mankind is further evidenced by its independence of any seasonal procreative urge as in animals, and its persistence when, through age or other cause, child-bearing is no longer possible.

But why, it may be asked, should this experience be between one man and one woman? Why should not this self-fulfilment be experienced with others? Here we touch one of the deep truths of spirit-fulfilment, which Christ both taught and also gave an example of it in His own life, when He said, 'I came, not to be ministered unto, but to minister.' True spirit-relationship has as its primary purpose, not self-fulfilment in another, but the fulfilment of the other in admitting him or her into intimate relation to oneself. In promiscuous sex-relationships there may be a feeling of self-fulfilment—it is often the justification put forward by those who indulge in them—but in the end it turns to disillusionment. True love, on the other hand, is the offering of oneself, both physically and spiritually, for the fulfilment of another, and in it there awakens more and more clearly the sense of one's own personal fulfilment. For the discovery is made of an ever deeper element in spirit-being, namely, that in the relationship between them, *each becomes part of the other's very being*. 'They are no more twain, but one', not only in the transient moments of physical union, but in this continually growing reality of spirit-relationship, in the sharing in each other's being in their life together. To break this relationship is to tear away part of the other's being.

All this is clearly expressed in the promises in the marriage service, in which each one says nothing of their own fulfilment or happiness, but offers himself or herself wholly to the fulfilment of the other. The conscious realization of this can give to those who are entering upon it a deep understanding of the meaning of Christian marriage, and in times of misunderstanding or disagreement can help each to form a truer conception of their own responsibility for it.

This conception of the spiritual union effected in marriage carries with it the demand, not only that it should be with one person, but also that it should be a lifelong relationship, and this is further established by other considerations.

In the first place, the whole purpose of man's earthly existence is that he should transmute his physical experience into spiritual experience. The physical union, if it is a true love-relationship, develops into a continuous intimate fellowship of mind and habit, which should ripen at the end of life into a pure unity of spirit. The finest testimony to the divine purpose in marriage is a love-relationship maintained undiminished into old age. It takes a lifetime together to attain to it.

Secondly, because man is spirit, his earthly life is not, as it is often taken to be, a day to day existence in which the past is lost and can be disregarded, and only the immediate present of sense-consciousness is real. Man's earthly life is the whole content of his earthly experience, in which nothing is left behind, and from which nothing is left out. That past self-offering in intimate physical and mental relationships, and all that followed from it, can never be expunged from the being of either partner. It is an ineradicable part of themselves, and carries for each of them inevitable consequences and responsibilities that do not end with death. The frailty or determination of either party may effect an earthly break with the past, but spiritually there is no escape from it. From an earthly point of view some people may face lightly the making and breaking of marriage after marriage, but from a spirit point of view they are creating a chaos of disrupted personal relationships, which they will one day have to face as all equally real. For every marriage, whatever the intent in making it, inevitably sets up enduring spiritual relationships.

Again, marriage needs to be a permanent relationship because others besides the married couple are inevitably involved in it. 'For this cause shall a man leave his father and his mother and cleave unto his wife.' These words imply that this 'making them male and female', this polarity of sex, had in its fulfilment a further purpose. It was to provide the true unit out of which human society was in the end to be fashioned, the unit of the freely chosen union of two persons in mutual love. Here again the formative spirit-pattern existed 'from the beginning', but it had to await any possibility of physical realization until there should awaken in man a real consciousness of self. Self-realization in love had to wait upon self-discovery in separatedness. Until then the marriage relationship was controlled by the physically evolving social units, family and tribe, and class and nation. Even until the end of the nineteenth century, in this country, a father's consent to his daughter's marriage was widely regarded as normal and necessary. Today the leaven is working more rapidly in the growing disregard by young people of any restriction of race or class or colour in mutual attraction. But if such marriages are to be the unit of a human society based on freedom and love, they must contain the permanent qualities of fidelity and selflessness.

Finally, marriage needs to be a lifelong relationship for out of it come children, other spirit-beings, whose chance of transforming self-discovery into self-fulfilment, and of themselves discharging in the future their own responsibilities as parents, will largely depend upon the atmosphere of their own parents' unselfish love for each other. The possibilities and responsibilities of marriage persist for every married couple through the three generations of a normal life.

Thus we see the deep significance and far-reaching effects of the relationship of marriage, implicit in that act of God 'in the beginning' to which Christ pointed. Deeply and widely as this relationship must involve others, Christ's words about marriage imply, as all feel when they fall in love, that it is first and foremost a relationship of two persons to each other, fulfilled physically in the sex act, divinely conceived to that end, and spiritually fulfilled in an intimacy of relationship closer than any other, and which can make possible to them, even on earth, the experience of their true being as spirit. This relationship between husband and wife is primary in marriage and an end in itself, and is not subordinate to nor always directed towards the biological end of procreation, though by the arrival of children it is deepened and strengthened in their common parenthood.

It is obvious that there are other human relationships into which men and women can enter, outside the marriage state, relationships which can be exalted to a real unity of spirit. But these can never be as entirely intimate as marriage, nor as creative in their external effect, nor as universal as marriage is made by the sex instinct implanted for that purpose in the whole race. The only human relationship which passes beyond the possibilities of marriage is the relation of the soul to God. It is to this that St Paul refers when he compares the relation between husband and wife to that between Christ and the Church; meaning, of course, by 'the Church' no formal institution, but the community of all human souls who in faith seek to know Christ in the intimacy of love. He speaks of it as 'a Mystery', a spiritual truth which the human mind cannot yet fully apprehend.

That such a relationship, which is both by its nature and its requirements lifelong, should be broken, is a tragedy of human failure. But it is not only broken by divorce. It is equally broken by a permanent legal separation. Marriage as Christ revealed it is not a divinely decreed status of union, but an actual continuous physical and spiritual intimacy of relationship. One who has promised to love and cherish and cleave to another in all circumstances, and invokes legal sanction to prevent the access of the other to their home or person, has renounced their marriage vow just as much as one who invokes legal authority, on the same grounds, to dissolve the union, which the action of his or her partner has deprived of its true content. In either case human frailty or wilfulness may have made the decision inevitable, but in both cases the spiritual unity is broken. Moreover, husband and wife who deliberately, year after year, live in continual strife or in mutual indifference, may not externally break their marriage union, but they continuously blaspheme against it.

It may well be asked, 'Why set out this exalted ideal of marriage, this spiritual purpose in it to which very few can attain and of which most men and women are completely unconscious? Why not accept the Christian teaching about the sanctity of marriage, and adjust it as best we may to the less exalted standard of the State?' The answer is that such an attitude will never solve the present situation between Church and State, in which men and women find themselves in a moral dilemma between their adherence to ecclesiastical regulations and the feeling that by them spiritual distress and injustice is inflicted upon individuals. Nor will it solve the present human perplexity about sex-relationship of which Berdyaev speaks.

The first need is for the Church herself to look again as deeply as possible into the spiritual significance of Christ's teaching, in such a way that she can reveal to mankind the actual spiritual realities involved in marriage. The nearest the Church comes to doing this is the definition of marriage in the marriage service as

'an honourable estate instituted of God in the time of man's innocency, signifying unto us the mystical union that is betwixt Christ and the Church'.

But this is not expounded or explained; it is merely given
expression in an alleged divine law of the indissolubility
of marriage. The description of the causes for which
matrimony was ordained, as the procreation of children,
the avoidance of the abuse of the sex-instinct, and the
mutual society, help, and comfort of husband and wife,
do not meet the desire, especially of the young, to understand what they feel is the strange mystery of the im-
mensely potent influence in human life of sex. It is a
definition at a completely different level from that of
marriage, as the God-intended physical and spiritual
fusion of two individuals, in order that they may experience
and bring to bear on others the true spirit-nature of their
being, as a fundamental factor in the spiritual evolution
of mankind.

If we ask why Christ defined marriage at this exalted,
almost unattainable level, instead of giving practical
rules about it which men could follow, the answer is that
that was the way in which Christ gave all His teaching.
When He taught of goodness He bade men to be perfect
as their Father in heaven is perfect; when He spoke of
purity, He defined it as the absence of any lustful thought;
when He spoke of man's responsibility for man, He said,
'Sell all your possessions and share them with others';
when He taught men goodwill, He said, 'Resist not him
that is evil'; when He spoke of generosity, He said,
'Lend to any would-be borrower and don't expect to
have your loan returned.'

It is often said that Christ taught with Eastern hyper-
bole, but there was far more in it than that. Christ revealed to men the pure spirit principles that are the
creative force behind the problems of conduct by which
mankind is faced. Man's search for goodness is not a

matter of imitation or emulation of earthly patterns, not a striving to reach the moral insight of Socrates or the strict religious observance of the Pharisees. It is in all men the divine pattern of goodness seeking to incarnate itself, through the intuitions of conscience, in the more or less responsive nature of human souls.

In doing this Christ served mankind in two ways. In the first place, He revealed the true pattern of evolution, namely, that man is raised, not by the half-conscious urge from below of physical necessity or expediency, but by the working in him, also half-consciously, of spiritual patterns of personal relationships, seeking to realize themselves in a physical setting. It is a truth man has yet to grasp and which he almost denies by his present outlook on evolution.

But in doing this Christ did more than give a revelation, He gave new power to these formative spirit patterns in their working upon the souls of man. By making conscious and living in the hearts of Christians the divine pattern of conduct, He released their transforming power into the world, even though they could not yet be realized in the physical setting. It was the sowing in men's hearts of the living Word, a creative ferment working from within. It was by those spirit-patterns, accepted by Christians as true though as yet unrealizable, that the moral standards of justice, compassion, human brotherhood, and the love of peace have reached a level, which no evolution from lower levels could have produced.

The tragedy arises when the ideals, which Christ released to be spiritual ferment in the hearts of men, are made into laws, immediately and rigidly applicable to existing human conditions, and binding here and now on men and women. Some made the divine standard of perfection a law, and held that one sin after baptism involved eternal punishment. Others try to set up communism or pacifism as immediately practical systems, binding on all Christians. So it is with marriage. The Christian teaching that marriage is a divinely-created fusion of a man and a woman in a lifelong union, that should only be ended by death and could never be dissolved at the will of husband or wife, was a ferment that in four centuries exalted the status of marriage in the Roman world. But the making of this ideal into a rigid law of the indissolubility of marriage, that has no mercy on the failure or misfortune of individuals, turned the creative working of an ideal into a straitjacket of compulsion, that took no account of man's moral imperfection and the social conditions under which he still had to live, and denied to the individual any possibility of making a second attempt to achieve the ideal.

Whenever we consider the application of Christ's moral and spiritual ideals, we must always remember that the most unique and startling revelation by Christ of God's attitude towards man's spiritual evolution was the possibility of absolute forgiveness for sin, and of a fresh start; and the refusal to subordinate the spiritual need of the individual to the strict application of the letter of the law.

The Christian ideal of marriage will not be preserved by the spiritual discipline of those who have failed to keep it and of those who are implicated in that failure; nor by making the creative act of God in marriage into the *ipse dixit* of a divine command. It can only be preserved by the Church penetrating to the spiritual purpose implicit in Christ's words, and making that the basis of her teaching about marriage; by imparting it pastorally to those who are finding it difficult to fulfil, in the way I have suggested; and by allowing to human failure a fresh start, blessed by God.

In this approach to the problem of marriage the Orthodox Church seems to succeed better than any other. Central to its faith and practice is the recognition of the sanctity and spiritual potentiality of the individual, and it regards as the primary quality of human relationships, especially within the Church, a deeply compassionate love of man for man. It holds marriage to be a calling of equal status with monasticism, and sets so high an ideal on the love of man and wife, as to regard it as ideally indissoluble even by death. A second, and still more a third, marriage is regarded as a declension from the ideal, and this is expressed in the marriage service itself, while a fourth marriage is forbidden.

But this ideal conception is never allowed to overwhelm compassion for those who have failed to achieve it, nor to refuse to them the opportunity of another attempt after divorce in remarriage. This attitude extends even to the guilty person, after a period of discipline, but for the innocent party there is only the subdued form of service that is used at all second marriages. The primary compassionate consideration of the individual is shown in the fact that, where either party is marrying for the first time, their innocence obliterates their partner's failure, and a full first-time ceremony is allowed. It is this mixture of extreme idealism with compassionate realism that enables the Orthodox Church to work with the State in the matter of marriage and divorce and, at the same time, to have a real influence on State legislation.

Although the Church of England has not that deep

mystic apprehension of the spiritual significance of love which is found in the Orthodox Church, she has, in her long-established belief in the spiritual freedom of the individual and in liberty of thought and interpretation, a quality that should enable her to make a special contribution to the solution of this problem. But, as we have seen, it is these freedoms that are threatened by the present Resolutions of Convocation. They can only be preserved by the refusal of clergy and lay people to be deprived of them, and by the watchfulness of Parliament in protecting, in any proposed legislation, the rights of individuals and minorities in the Established Church.

Our consideration, in this chapter, of the purposes for which marriage was made for man by God 'in the beginning', has revealed levels of experience which few would claim to have reached, but which, once realized, can be an inspiration to all who seek to fulfil the ideals and intents with which they entered into marriage. It is seen to be a spiritual relationship between husband and wife, the breaking of which must always be a spiritual tragedy, even if it is the inescapable result of human weakness or sinfulness. But it is only by combining with this exalted concept of marriage our instinctive English belief in the right of individuals to be free from spiritual coercion or deprivation in following the dictates of their own conscience, that the Church can help the nation to solve this problem of which it is so deeply conscious. As in the Orthodox Church, the mystery of the divine ideal of marriage must be interwoven with the mystery of the divine compassion.